P9-AFO-803

WITHDRAWN
UTSA Libraries

Index to Translated
Short Fiction by
Latin American Women
in English Language
Anthologies

Recent Titles in
Bibliographies and Indexes in Women's Studies

Index to Translated Short Fiction by Latin American Women in English Language Anthologies

Compiled by
KATHY S. LEONARD

Bibliographies and Indexes in Women's Studies,
Number 25

GREENWOOD PRESS
Westport, Connecticut • London

University of Texas
at San Antonio

Library of Congress Cataloging-in-Publication Data

Index to translated short fiction by Latin American women in English
   language anthologies / compiled by Kathy S. Leonard.
       p.   cm.—(Bibliographies and indexes in women's studies,
   ISSN 0742–6941 ; no. 25)
   Includes bibliographical references and index.
   ISBN 0–313–30046–1 (alk. paper)
   1. Latin American fiction—Women authors—Translations into
English—Indexes. 2. Short stories, Latin American—Translations
into English—Indexes. 3. Latin American fiction—20th century
—Translations into English—Indexes. I. Leonard, Kathy S., 1952– .
II. Series.
Z1609.F4I6   1997
[PQ7082.S5]
863—dc21   97–33141

British Library Cataloguing in Publication Data is available.

Copyright © 1997 by Kathy S. Leonard

All rights reserved. No portion of this book may be
reproduced, by any process or technique, without the
express written consent of the publisher.

Library of Congress Catalog Card Number: 97–33141
ISBN: 0–313–30046–1
ISSN: 0742–6941

First published in 1997

Greenwood Press, 88 Post Road West, Westport, CT 06881
An imprint of Greenwood Publishing Group, Inc.

Printed in the United States of America

The paper used in this book complies with the
Permanent Paper Standard issued by the National
Information Standards Organization (Z39.48–1984).

10 9 8 7 6 5 4 3 2

Library
University of Texas
at San Antonio

Contents

Acknowledgments

I would like to gratefully acknowledge the following sources of support that made the preparation of this book possible: Iowa State University for awarding me a Faculty Improvement Leave which provided the time to work on this manuscript; the Department of Education, Cornell/Pittsburgh Consortium, for awarding me a Research Fellowship/Visiting Scholar appointment to Cornell University which enabled me to use the collections at Olin Library; and the Inter-library Loan Department at Iowa State University for their efficient handling of hundreds of requests. Individuals who helped with the various stages of the manuscript include Isabel Izquierdo, my research assistant, and Karina Shea and Barbara Dyer, who helped with data input, computer-related questions, and manuscript corrections. As always, I am grateful to Michael Porter for reviewing all portions of the manuscript as well as for his continued moral support throughout the research and writing process.

Preface

Introduction

During the past ten years there has been a dramatic change in the situation of women writers in Latin America as well as in the interest the reading public has shown in their work worldwide. In the United States, much of this heightened interest coincided with the formation of women's studies programs in American universities, programs which have often challenged the prevailing notion of what is considered worthy of scholarly interest and analysis. Consequently, many works of literature written by women have gained new respect and attention.

This new-found status in women's literature has caused publishers to take note, dramatically increasing the number of works by Latin American women writers being published, not only in their own countries, but also in the United States and Britain, where novels and collections of short stories are appearing in the original Spanish as well as in English translation. Among these publishers are a number of important academic presses, which include the University of Nebraska Press, that has a Latin American Women Writers series, and the University of Texas, which publishes women's work in their Texas Pan-American series. Another important publisher of women's writing is the Latin American Literary Review Press, which specializes in the publishing of popular and scholarly books on Latin American subjects, most of them translations of important Latin American literary work. The Latin American Literary Review Press has recently published a number of both well-known and unknown women authors in their series titled Discoveries, among them, Jacqueline Balcells (Chile), Julieta Campos, Angelina Muñiz-Huberman, and Rosario Castellanos (Mexico), and Carmen Naranjo and Rima de Vallbona (Costa Rica). Smaller presses also active in this area include White Pine Press, with its Secret Weavers list directed by Marjorie Agosín, Curbstone Press, Westview Press, Cleis Press, and Aunt Lute, all of which have published a number of titles by Latin American women writers.

The large trade presses of New York have begun to follow suit, with several of them seeking out work by Chicana, Latina, and Latin American women writers. These publishers are most often interested in novel-length works, but will occasionally publish a novella or collection of short stories if the authors are well known. This is evidenced by such works as *Out of the Mirrored Garden*, published in 1996 by Doubleday (an Anchor Book), a volume that contains such authors as Elena Poniatowska, Rosario Ferré, and Elena Castedo. However, the novel seems to be the preferred choice for these publishing houses, and we have many examples of their products. The translation of Laura Esquivel's novel *Like Water for Chocolate* was published by Doubleday in 1992, and became a best seller. Isabel Allende, perhaps one of the best known of the Latin American women authors, has had all of her novels translated into English and published with other big-name publishing houses in New York: *The Infinite Plan: A Novel*, and *Paula*, both published by HarperCollins; *Of Love and Shadows* and *The House of the Spirits* were published by Knopf. Vintage Books, which is a division of Random House, as is Knopf, has a Spanish language division called Vintage Español that publishes well-known Latin American authors, male and female. Among their women authors are the Mexican writers Angeles Mastretta (*Mexican Bolero*, 1989) and Carmen Boullosa (*The Miracle-worker*, 1995). Vintage also publishes Spanish translations of popular works which were originally written in English. These include Esmeralda Santiago's *When I Was Puerto Rican* and Sandra Cisneros' *The House on Mango Street*.

Purpose

Work on this volume was originally initiated from a personal need. While researching materials to be translated and included in an anthology of short stories by women authors from Bolivia, Ecuador, and Peru, I wished to know if stories I had selected had been previously translated. I discovered that no definitive work of such information existed. Although there are a variety of bibliographies available which include a smattering of entries of short fiction by women authors in translation, no index such as I present here was available.

My intent with this volume is to give scholars, researchers, instructors, and students access to a complete, or a very nearly complete, listing of short fiction by Latin American women in translation, with the hope that these works will be read, incorporated into the curriculum of courses in Latin American literature, ethnic studies, women's studies, and other courses where matters of Latin America are of interest.

Organization

The reader will find five indices within this volume. The principal index is titled "Anthology Index," and it is organized and listed according to the author or editor of the anthology in alphabetical order. A code number appears alongside each entry. For example, the number A1 refers to the first entry of the "Anthology

Index" which is Agosín, Marjorie, the author of the work listed. These code numbers are cross-referenced throughout the other indices, referring the reader back to the principal index where the work in question can be found. The annotation for each entry includes all bibliographic information as well as a list of all works of short fiction and novel excerpts by Latin American women authors which appear within the volume. The author's country of birth follows her name in parenthesis. If the anthology is the work of a single author, country information appears immediately after her name and her works are listed as they appear in her book, which may or may not be in alphabetical order. If the anthology includes a number of writers, the authors are listed in alphabetical order according to their surname, with the title(s) of their works following. Some of the author surnames may show variations in spelling, for example, Carmen Lira/Lyra, and Liliana Hecker/Heker. In the "Anthology Index," authors' names appear exactly as published. In the other indices, such as in the "Alphabetical Author Index," names with variations in spelling are listed twice: Lira/Lyra and Lyra/Lira, as they fall in alphabetical order.

A number of the stories published in the anthologies have been translated more than once, by different translators, and thus may show variations in their titles from one anthology to another. For example, a story by Luisa Valenzuela is titled "The Snow White Guard" in one anthology (A4), and "The Snow White Watchman" in two others (V1, V3). All titles are listed within the indices exactly as they appear in the anthologies. Some of the anthologies are bilingual, and in such cases, the title of the story is listed in English and Spanish, with the Spanish title following in parentheses. For example, "Sincronio, The Bird of Wonder (Sincronio, el ave fénix)."

The four other indices included within this volume are: "Alphabetical Author Index," "Author by Country Index," "Title Index," and "Authors and Their Works Index." There is a great deal of repetition and overlap among the indices, which is intentional. As a researcher, I found many of the bibliographies I consulted difficult to work with due to the constant necessity to flip from one index to another. I have organized this work for ease of use, and each index provides a variety of information, often eliminating the need to refer to the others. If the reader is searching for a particular author name, he/she may find it listed in alphabetical order in the "Alphabetical Author Index" or by country of birth in the "Author by Country Index." If the reader is searching for a particular title, it may be found in the"Title Index," which contains all the works listed in alphabetical order along with the author's name and the code number referring back to the "Anthology Index." A reader interested in locating all works by a particular author can find them in the "Authors and Their Works Index."

Concerning alphabetization of author names, there are a number of surnames which begin with "de" or "de la", as in Giancarla de Quiroga or Teresa de la Parra. When alphabetizing such names, the convention in Hispanic countries is to list them thusly: Quiroga, Giancarla de. I have chosen to list these names under "D" considering the "de" the first element in the last name. This approach is taken due to the nature of the work, which I feel may be consulted primarily by readers who may not be speakers of Spanish and may not be familiar with the conventions of alphabetization of Spanish surnames. If this organization causes undue confusion, it will be corrected in following editions.

The Works Cited chapter includes a list of bibliographies consulted in the preparation of this volume. However, a variety of other sources were consulted, including on-line library databases throughout the United States, which often did not include recently published works, prompting frequent visits to bookstores, local and otherwise.

Scope

This volume includes indices of short stories, short fiction, and novel excerpts written by Latin American women authors, including those from Brazil, translated into English from either Spanish or Portuguese. These works were culled from 165 anthologies published between the years of 1938 and 1996. Many of the anthologies included here contain an overwhelming number of works by male authors, works which I have chosen not to include, feeling that their inclusion would detract from the purpose of this volume.

This index includes short fiction published in anthologies only; it does not include short stories published individually in periodicals or literary journals, with the three exceptions noted here. I have listed two issues of *Mundus Artium*: 8.2, "International Short Fiction," and 7.2, "International Women's Issue," as well as one issue of *Evergreen Review* 2.7 "The Eye of Mexico," since these special issues were published in anthology format.

Some of the anthologies listed in the index contain work by non-Latin American women writers who may be of interest to readers, especially to university instructors in courses of women's studies. One such anthology is *The Longman Anthology of Literature by Women, 1875-1975*, (A13), which also contains a lengthy introduction dealing with women's literature and essays concerning women's literature in a number of countries. This information appears in the annotation.

Although I have included information on other women writers when appropriate, in the indices themselves, only work by "Latin American" authors is listed, and only, with a few exceptions, work which has been translated from either Spanish or Portuguese. Many of the anthologies also include work by either "Latina" or "Chicana" writers, which after some deliberation, I decided not to include since most Chicana and Latina authors write in English. Nonetheless, a number of anthologies combine the work of Latina, Chicana, and Latin American authors into the category of "Latina," as occurs in *Daughters of the Fifth Sun: A Collection of Latina Fiction and Poetry*, (M16), which makes it difficult to determine an author's identity and to ascertain the original language of her story. Many Latin American-born authors now reside in the United States and they may or may not write in English and they may or may not refer to themselves as

"Latina" or be classified as such when their work is included in an anthology. Such authors include Elena Castedo (born in Spain and raised in Chile) who writes in English and whose work has then been translated into Spanish. There are also Julia Alvarez (Dominican), Judith Ortiz Cofer (Puerto Rican), both of whom write in English, and Marjorie Agosín (Chilean), who has lived in the United States since her high school years but who writes in Spanish. After giving the matter much consideration, I made the decision to include work which was originally written in Spanish or Portuguese and then translated into English (with a few exceptions, which are noted as having been originally written in English, if such information is known). Within these limitations, some of the confusing categorization of authors is erased. However, an updated version of this index (already in the planning) will also include, in a separate index, anthologies of work in English by Latin American and Latina authors which was originally written in English. This would allow for the inclusion of books such as *Little Havana Blues: A Cuban-American Literature Anthology*, which contains works by Cuban-born authors who write in English while residing in the United States. Such volumes of literature are becoming increasingly more abundant and should not be overlooked in indices.

Some types of work which might be considered short fiction, specifically folktales or stories based on oral traditions, are not included in this volume. My intent is for the reader to become familiar with the work of specific authors, and typically, folktales and oral stories are anonymous. On the other hand, I have included work which does not fit neatly into the category of short fiction. This includes writing by the Brazilian Clarice Lispector; her book *The Foreign Legion*, (L5), contains a number of short stories, but also includes "Chronicles," which consist of art criticism, travel notes, and personal reflections. Nellie Campobello's *Cartucho* is referred to as a novel, but it actually consists of fifty-six sketches made up of autobiography, history, and poetry. Her work *My Mother's Hands* is described as a poem by its translator. However, its format is that of short fictional pieces. Marjorie Agosín's work also defies neat categorization, since it often consists of lyrical prose pieces that seem to be more poetry than prose. Pieces which were obviously poems were excluded from the index, but pieces having the appearance of prose, or which seemed to be more prose than poetry, were included. I have listed these works and others of a similar nature, preferring to err on the side of caution for fear of excluding pieces which might be of use or interest to readers.

Some of the works included here are intended for specific audiences, e.g., Maricarmen O'hara's *Cuentos para todos/Tales for Everybody*, (O2), which is essentially a reader designed to teach Spanish to adult learners. While some may argue that her stories are not true pieces of literature, they do fall within the guidelines of this volume.

There has been no attempt to group the works included here by theme, although many of the anthologies themselves are organized in such a manner. The most common organization of anthologies is by country, and anthologies organized along those lines include *What Is Secret: Stories by Chilean Women*, (A5), *Bridges to Cuba. Puentes a Cuba*, (B4), *Rhythm and Revolt: Tales of the Antilles*, (B13), and *Contistas brasileiros. New Brazilian Short Stories,* (C13). Anthologies organized by thematic content include *Secret Weavers: Stories of the Fantastic by Women of Argentina and Chile,* (A6), *Pleasure in the Word: Erotic Writing by Latin American Women,* (F3), *Nature's Ban. Women's Incest Literature,* (J1), and *Cruel Fictions, Cruel Realities: Short Stories by Latin American Women,* (L1). However, the majority of the anthologies simply gather into one volume a variety of writers, whose only commonality is that of being designated as Latin American. Within those anthologies, the thematic content of the stories varies dramatically; the reader will encounter everything from simple love stories to graphic exposés of political corruption.

Conclusion

Many new anthologies were surfacing as I completed the preparation of this book. I was torn between including them, and causing myself a great deal of revision work, thus jeopardizing completing the manuscript by its deadline, or leaving the new anthologies for inclusion in a revised edition of this work. I decided on the latter.

I personally reviewed all anthologies listed here and take full responsibility for the contents of this volume, including any errors or unintentional omissions. All suggestions for corrections or inclusion of works for a second edition are greatly appreciated.

I

Anthology Index

A1   Agosín, Marjorie (Chile). *Happiness: Stories by Marjorie Agosín.* Trans. and intro. Elizabeth Horan. Fredonia: White Pine Press, 1993. 237 pp.

Short Stories:
Slaves; Happiness; Fat; Braids; An Immense Black Umbrella; Adelina; Nana; Monserrat Ordóñez; Emma; Wax Candles; Gypsy Women; North; Photographs; The Gold Bracelet; The Fiesta; Orphanages; The Seamstress from Saint Petersburg; The Eiderdown; Pisagua; The Hen; Pork Sausages; Itinerants; Water; Signs of Love; Love Letters; First Time to the Sea; Mirrors; Meditation on the Dead; Río de la Plata; Blood; Journey to the End of Coasts; Forests; Beds; Cartographies; The Dead; The Rubber Tree; Long Live Life; Prairies; Sargasso; Rivers; Distant Root of Autumn Loves; Naked; Houses by the Sea; The Dreams of Van Gogh.

A2   ___. *Women in Disguise: Stories by Marjorie Agosín.* Trans. Diane Russell-Pineda. Falls Church: Azul Editions, 1996. 164 pp.

Short Stories:
Chapter I, Women Potters: Curriculum Vitae (poem); Last Names; Silences; Convents; Strip Tease; Olga; Letters; Bonfires; Guillermina Aguilar; The Cemetery; Alfama. Chapter II, Ritual:2 First Communion; Women in Disguise; Cousins; The Messiah; Chepita; Birthday; Weddings. Chapter III, In September, When the Rains Stop: The Alphabet; Dunedin; Ireland; Chocolates; The Wanderer; Islands; Ocean Retreats; Allison. Chapter IV, Death Sounds: The Place I Want to Die; Lady Death; Rivers; Antigua; Warnings; Spirits; House of Lights; Widowhood; Appointment; Death Sounds; The Color Black. Chapter V, Tickle of Love: Revenge; Fingertips (poem); This Love; A Scented Love Letter; The Bottle; A

Recent Nakedness; Life Inside of Love; Tickle of Love. Chapter VI, Bougainvillaea Insomnia: Dreamer of Fishes; Pine Trees; The Tower; Postcards; Mists; Bougainvillaea Insomnia; Witches; Wine.

This volume is a reworking of Agosín's book *Las alfareras*. Some texts have been added, others deleted. Includes a foreword by Patricia Rubio.

A3   **Agosín, Marjorie, ed. and intro. *A Gabriela Mistral Reader.* Trans. Maria Giachetti. Fredonia: White Pine Press, 1993. 227 pp.**

Prose Selections:
Gabriela Mistral (Chile), The Sea; The Body; In Praise of Gold; The Lark; In Praise of Small Towns; In Praise of Stones; The Giraffe; An Owl; The Alpaca; The Coconut Palms; In Praise of Salt; Flour; The Little New Moon; Bread; The Fig.

This volume also includes poetry and essays written by Mistral. Agosín's introduction titled "Gabriela Mistral, the Restless Soul," deals with Mistral's life and works.

A4   **___, ed. and intro. *Landscapes of a New Land: Short Fiction by Latin American Women.* Fredonia: White Pine Press, 1993. 193 pp.**

Short Stories:
Dora Alonso (Cuba), Cage Number One. **Helena Araujo** (Colombia), The Open Letter. **Jacqueline Balcells** (Chile), The Enchanted Raisin. **Yolanda Bedregal** (Bolivia), "Good Evening, Agatha." **Patricia Bins** (Brazil), Destination. **María Luisa Bombal** (Chile), Sky, Sea and Earth. **Marta Brunet** (Chile), Solitude of Blood. **Lygia Fagundes Telles** (Brazil), The Key. **Margo Glantz** (Mexico), Genealogies. **Hilda Hilst** (Brazil), An Avid One in Extremis; Natural Theology. **Clarice Lispector** (Brazil), Plaza Mauá. **Carmen Naranjo** (Costa Rica), The Compulsive Couple of the House on the Hill. **Silvina Ocampo** (Argentina), The Servant's Slaves. **Elvira Orphée** (Argentina), The Beguiling Ladies. **Cristina Peri Rossi** (Uruguay), The Museum of Futile Endeavors. **Nélida Piñón** (Brazil), I Love My Husband. **Elena Poniatowska** (Mexico), The Message. **Amalia Rendic** (Chile), A Child, a Dog, the Night. **Laura Riesco** (Peru), Jimena's Fair. **Alicia Steimberg** (Argentina), Cecilia's Last Will and Testament. **Luisa Valenzuela** (Argentina), The Snow White Guard.

Includes brief bio-bibliographic notes on authors and translators.

A5   **___, ed. and intro. *What Is Secret: Stories by Chilean Women.***

Fredonia: White Pine Press, 1995. 303 pp.

Short Stories:
Margarita Aguirre, Cleaning the Closet. **Elena Aldunate**, Butterfly Man. **María Flor Aninat**, The Department Store. **Jacqueline Balcells**, The Boy Who Took Off in a Tree. **Pía Barros**, Scents of Wood and Silence. **Carmen Basáñez**, Not Without Her Glasses. **Alejandra Basualto**, A Requiem for Hands. **Marta Blanco**, Maternity. **María Luisa Bombal**, The Secret. **Marta Brunet**, Down River. **Elena Castedo**, The White Bedspread. **Cristina da Fonseca**, Memories of Clay; Endless Flight. **María Asunción De Fokes**, Vanessa and Victor. **Ana María del Río**, Subway. **Alejandra Farias**, The Fish Tank. **Agata Gligo**, The Bicycles. **Sonia González Valdenegro**, A Matter of Distance. **Lucía Guerra**, Encounter on the Margins. **Ana María Güiraldes**, Up to the Clouds; The Family Album. **Sonia Guralnik**, Sailing Down the Rhine. **Marta Jara**, The Dress; The Englishwoman. **Luz Larraín**, The Bone Spoon. **Sonia Montecinos**, Hualpín. **Barbara Mujica**, Mitrani. **Margarita Niemeyer**, The House. **Luz Orfanoz**, Insignificance; Accelerated Cycle. **Ana Pizarro**, The Journey. **Violeta Quevedo**, The Pilgrim's Angel. **Amalia Rendic**, A Dog, a Boy, and the Night. **Elizabeth Subercaseaux**, Because We're Poor. **Ana Vásquez**, Elegance. **Virginia Vidal**, Journey of the Watermelon. **María Flora Yáñez**, The Pond.

Includes bio-bibliographic notes on authors and translators.

A6 **Agosín, Marjorie, and Celeste Kostopulos-Cooperman, eds.** *Secret Weavers: Stories of the Fantastic by Women of Argentina and Chile.* Fredonia: White Pine Press, 1993. 339 pp.

Short Fiction:
Isabel Allende (Chile), Two Words. **María Luisa Bombal** (Chile), The Story of María Griselda. **Alina Diaconú** (Argentina), The Storm; Welcome to Albany; The Widower. **Marosa Di Giorgio** (Uruguay), excerpts from *The Wild Papers*. **Sara Gallardo** (Argentina), The Man in the Araucaria; The Blue Stone Emperor's Thirty Wives. **Angélica Gorodischer** (Argentina), The Perfect Married Woman; Letters From an English Lady; Under the Flowering Juleps; The Resurrection of the Flesh. **Liliana Hecker** (Argentina), When Everything Shines. **Luisa Mercedes Levinson** (Argentina), The Little Island; The Boy Who Saw God's Tears. **Silvina Ocampo** (Argentina), The Compulsive Dreamer; Things; The Velvet Dress; The House of Sugar; Thus Were Their Faces. **Olga Orozco** (Argentina), For Friends and Enemies; And the Wheel Still Spins. **Elvira Orphée** (Argentina), An Eternal Fear; I Will Return, Mommy; How the Little Crocodiles Cry. **Cristina Peri Rossi** (Uruguay), The Annunciation.

Alejandra Pizarnik (Argentina), The Mirror of Melancholy; Blood Baths; Severe Measures. **Ana María Shua** (Argentina), excerpts from *Dream Time:* Other/Other; Fishing Days. **Marcela Solá** (Argentina), The Condemned Dress in White; Happiness; Invisible Embroidery. **Alicia Steimberg** (Argentina), Viennese Waltz; García's Thousandth Day; Segismundo's Better World. **Elizabeth Subercaseaux** (Chile), Selections from *Silendra*: Tapihue; Enedina; Juana; Silendra; Francisco. **Luisa Valenzuela** (Argentina), Country Carnival; Legend of the Self-Sufficient Child.

Includes an introduction by Marjorie Agosín, "Reflections on the Fantastic."

A7   **Ahern, Maureen, ed. and intro. *A Rosario Castellanos Reader*. Austin: University of Texas Press, 1988. 378 pp.**

Short Fiction:
Rosario Castellanos (Mexico).   The Eagle; Three Knots in the Net; Fleeting Friendships; *The Widower Román* (novella); Cooking Lesson.

Includes brief bio-bibliographic notes on the editor and the translators.

A8   **Ahern, Tom, ed. *Diana's Second Almanac*. Providence: Diana's Bimonthly Press, 1980. 88 pp.**

Short Stories:
Armonía Somers (Uruguay), The Immigrant.

A9   **Alegría, Claribel (El Salvador). *Family Album*. Trans. Amanda Hopkinson. Willimantic: Curbstone Press, 1991. 191 pp.**

Novellas:
The Talisman; Family Album; Village of God and the Devil.

A10   **___. *Luisa in Realityland*. Trans. Darwin J. Flakoll. Willimantic: Curbstone Press, 1987. 152 pp.**

Short Stories:
Wilf (1); Luisa's Litanies; Wilf (2); Luisa and the Gypsy; Wilf (3); Aunt Elsa and Cuis; I'm a Whore: Are You Satisfied?; The Ancestor Room; Taking the Vows; The Versailles Tenement; The President's Sheet; The Nicaraguan Great-Grandfather (1); First Communion; The Nicaraguan Grandfather (2); Aunt Filiberta and Her Cretonnes; The Nicaraguan Grandfather (3); The Myth-making Uncles (1); Rene; Margarita's Birthday;

Felix; Jane's Umbilical Cord; Cipitio; Jamie in Poneloya; The Day of the Cross; The Gypsy (1); Luisa's Paintings; The Gypsy (2); Premature Necrology; The Deaf Mutes of Ca'n Blau; The Flood; Sunday Siestas; The Mad Woman of the Grand Armee; Roque's Via Crucis; The Myth-making Uncles (2); Farabundo Marti; Nightmare in Chinandega; Granny and the Golden Bridge; Prophecy (1); The Singer Machines; The Blue Theatre; Eunice Aviles; Appointment in Zinica; The Gypsy (3); The Pool; Salarrue; Plash, Plash, Plash; No Dogs or Mexicans; The Mejia's Dogs; Carmen Bomba; Poet; Prophecy (2); The Gypsy (4); Final Act.

This volume also includes poetry and brief bio-bibliographic notes on the author.

A11   Allende, Isabel (Chile). *The Stories of Eva Luna*. Trans. Margaret Sayers Peden. New York: Atheneum, 1991. 331 pp.

Short Stories:
Two Words; Wicked Girl; Clarisa; Toad's Mouth; The Gold of Tomás Vargas; If You Touched My Heart; Gift for a Sweetheart; Tosca; Wilimai; Ester Lucero; Simple María; Our Secret; The Little Heidelberg; The Judge's Wife; The Road North; The Schoolteacher's Guest; The Proper Respect; Interminable Life; A Discreet Miracle; Revenge; Letters of Betrayed Love; Phantom Palace; And of Clay Are We Created.

Includes a prologue by Rolf Carlé.

A12   Allgood, Myralyn F., ed., preface, intro., and trans. *Another Way to Be: Selected Works of Rosario Castellanos* (Mexico). Athens: The University of Georgia Press, 1990. 146 pp.

Short Fiction:
Three Knots in the Net; The Nine Guardians (excerpt from *Balún Canán*); The Luck of Teodoro Méndez Acúbal; The Cycle of Hunger; Tenebrae Service (excerpt from *Oficio de tinieblas)*; Cooking Lesson.

Includes a foreword by Edward D. Terry and an extensive bibliography of primary and secondary works for Rosario Castellanos in Spanish and English.

A13   Arkin, Marian, and Barbara Shollar, eds. *Longman Anthology of Literature by Women, 1875-1975*. New York: Longman, 1989. 1274 pp.

Short Fiction:
María Luisa Bombal (Chile), Braids. **Lydia Cabrera** (Cuba), Walo-Wila. **Nellie Campobello** (Mexico), excerpt from *Cartridge: Tales of the Struggle in Northern Mexico*. **Carolina María de Jesús** (Brazil), excerpt from *Child of the Dark*. **Teresa de la Parra** (Venezuela), No More Mill, excerpt from *Mama Blanca's Souvenirs*. **Rachel de Queiroz** (Brazil), excerpt from *The Three Marías*. **Rosario Ferré** (Puerto Rico), The Youngest Doll. **Luisa Josefina Hernández** (Mexico), Florinda and Don Gonzalo. **Clarice Lispector** (Brazil), The Beginnings of a Fortune. **Carmen Lyra** (Costa Rica), prologue to *The Tales of My Aunt Panchita*. **Clorinda Matto de Turner** (Peru), excerpt from *Birds Without a Nest*. **Cristina Peri Rossi** (Uruguay), The Trapeze Artists. **Nélida Piñón** (Brazil), Bird of Paradise. **Elena Poniatowska** (Mexico), Love Story. **Luisa Valenzuela** (Argentina), Strange Things Happen Here. **Leonor Villegas de Magnon** (Mexico), excerpt from *The Rebellious Woman*.

Includes a lengthy introduction concerning women's literature. The appendices contain essays dealing with women's literary traditions from each country represented in the anthology; the essay on Spanish America was written by Margarite Fernández Olmos. Includes an index of writers and selections by region.

A14   **Arredondo, Inés (Mexico). *Underground River and Other Stories*. Trans. and intro. Cynthia Steele. Lincoln: University of Nebraska Press, 1996. 128 pp.**

Short Stories:
The Shunammite; Mariana; The Sign; New Year's Eve; Underground River; The Silent Words; Orphanhood; The Nocturnal Butterflies; The Brothers; The Mirrors; On Love; Shadow in the Shadows.

Includes a foreword by Elena Poniatowska.

B1   **Balcells, Jacqueline (Chile). *The Enchanted Raisin*. Trans. Elizabeth Gamble Miller. Pittsburgh: Latin American Literary Review Press, 1988. 103 pp.**

Short Stories:
The Enchanted Raisin; The Mermaids' Elixir; The Buried Giant; The Princess and the Green Dwarf; How Forgetfulness Began; The Boy Swept Away in a Tree; The Thirsty Little Fish.

Children's stories and fairy tales.

B2   Bandiera Duarte, Margarida Estrela (Brazil). *Legend of the Palm Tree*. New York: Grosset and Dunlap, 1940. 47 pp.

B3   Barros, Pía (Chile). *Transitory Fears*. Trans. Diane Russell-Pineda and Martha Manier. Santiago: Asterión Publishers, 1989. 176 pp.

Short Stories:
Abelardo; Story for a Window; Estanvito; Appraisals; Coup; No Circles; Waiting Game; Short-lived Summers; The Baby's Afternoon; Windows; Horses are a Gringo Invention; Portal; When the Patagonians Hunted Stars; Routine Inspection; Messages; Looking at Manet; Núñez from Over Here; The Inheritor of Wisdom; Shoes.

Bilingual edition. Includes bio-bibliographic notes on author and translators.

B4   Behar, Ruth, ed. and intro. *Bridges to Cuba. Puentes a Cuba.* Ann Arbor: University of Michigan Press, 1995. 421 pp.

Short Fiction:
Teresa Marrero, Ghost Limbs. **Rita Martín**, Elisa, or the Price of Dreams.

Includes brief bio-bibliographic information on contributors.

B5   Benner, Susan, and Kathy S. Leonard, eds., trans., and intro. *Fire from the Andes: Short Fiction by Women from Bolivia, Ecuador, and Peru.* Albuquerque: University of New Mexico Press, 1997.

Short Fiction:
Virginia Ayllón Soria (Bolivia), Prayer to the Goddesses. **Yolanda Bedregal** (Bolivia), The Traveler. **Mónica Bravo** (Ecuador), Wings for Dominga. **Erika Bruzonic** (Bolivia), Inheritance. **Aminta Buenaño** (Ecuador), The Strange Invasion that Rose from the Sea. **Gaby Cevasco** (Peru), Between Clouds and Lizards. **Giancarla de Quiroga** (Bolivia), Of Anguish and Illusions. **Elsa Dorado de Revilla Valenzuela** (Bolivia), The Parrot. **Pilar Dughi** (Peru), The Days and Hours. **María del Carmen Garcés** (Ecuador), The Blue Handkerchief. **Carmen Luz Gorriti** (Peru), The Legacy (A Story from Huancayo). **Bethzabé Guevara** (Peru), The Señorita Didn't Teach Me. **Marcela Gutiérrez** (Bolivia), The Feathered Serpent. **Beatriz Kuramoto** (Bolivia), The Agreement. **Beatriz Loayza Millán** (Bolivia), The Mirror. **Catalina Lohman** (Peru), The Red Line. **Nela Martínez** (Ecuador), La Machorra. **Mónica Ortiz Salas** (Ecuador), Mery Yagual (Secretary). **Blanca Elena Paz** (Bolivia), The Light. **Laura**

Riesco (Peru), The Twins of Olmedo Court. **Gladys Rossel Huicí** (Peru), Light and Shadow. **Fabiola Solís de King** (Ecuador), Before It's Time. **Eugenia Viteri** (Ecuador), The Ring. **Alicia Yánez Cossío** (Ecuador), The Mayor's Wife.

Includes biographic information, a photograph, and a primary and secondary bibliography for each author. Also includes an extensive bibliography titled "Short Story Collections by or Including Women Authors from Bolivia, Ecuador, and Peru." Foreword by Marjorie Agosín and notes on the editors/translators.

B6   Biddle, Arthur, ed., intro., and preface. *Global Voices: Contemporary Literature from the Non-western World.* **Englewood Cliffs: Prentice Hall, A Blair Press Book, 1995. 845 pp.**

         Short Stories:
         Rosario Ferré (Puerto Rico), The Youngest Doll. **Luisa Valenzuela** (Argentina), The Censors.

B7   **Bohner, Charles H., ed. and intro.** *Short Fiction: Classic and Contemporary.* **3rd. ed. Englewood Cliffs: Prentice Hall, 1994. 1183 pp.**

         Short Stories:
         Luisa Valenzuela (Argentina), The Verb *to Kill.*

         Includes bio-bibliographic notes on authors. This volume is intended for use in college courses.

B7.1   **Bojunga-Nunes, Lygia (Brazil).** *The Companions.* **Trans. Ellen Watson. New York: Farrar, Straus, & Giroux, 1984. 58 pp.**

         Short Stories:
         Fast Friends; A Time of Trouble; Summer.

         Children's stories. Illustrated by Larry Wilkes.

B7.2   ___. *My Friend the Painter.* **Trans. Giovanni Pontiero. San Diego: Harcourt Brace Jovanovich, Publishers. 85 pp.**

         A children's story.

B8   **Bombal, María Luisa (Chile).** *New Islands and Other Stories.* **Trans. Richard and Lucía Cunningham. New York: Farrar, Straus &**

Giroux, 1982. 112 pp.

Short Stories:
The Final Mist; The Tree; Braids; The Unknown; New Islands.

Includes a brief preface by Jorge Luís Borges.

B9   **Borges, Jorge Luís, Silvina Ocampo, and Adolfo Bioy Casares, eds.**
     The Book of Fantasy. **New York: Viking, 1988. 384 pp.**

Short Stories:
Elena Garro (Mexico), A Secure Home. **Delia Ingenieros** and **Jorge Luís Borges** (Argentina), Odin. **Silvina Ocampo** (Argentina), The Atonement.

Includes a brief introduction by Ursula K. Le Guin and very brief bio-bibliographic notes on authors.

B10   **Bowen, David, and Juan A. Ascencio, eds.** *Pyramids of Glass: Short Fiction from Modern Mexico.* **San Antonio: Corona Publishing Co., 1994. 244 pp.**

Short Stories:
Inés Arredondo, Puzzles. **Marta Cerda**, Mirror of a Man. **Guadalupe Dueñas**, Mariquita and Me. **Silvia Molina**, An Orange is an Orange. **Angeles Mastretta**, White Lies. **Elena Poniatowska**, Little House of Celluloid. **María Luisa Puga**, The Trip.

Includes an introduction by Ilan Stavans and bio-bibliographic notes on contributors.

B11   **Boyce Davies, Carole E., and 'Molara Ogundipe-Leslie, eds and intro.**
     Moving Beyond Boundaries. Volume 1: International Dimensions of Black Women's Writing. **New York: New York University Press, 1995. 252 pp.**

Short Stories:
Luz Argentina Chiriboga (Ecuador), Under the Skin of the Drums (excerpt from the novel *Bajo la piel de los tambores*).

Inclues a brief preface by Carole Boyce Davies, bio-bibliographic notes on authors, and two introductions: "Hearing Black Women's Voices: Transgressing Imposed Boundaries," by Carole E. Boyce Davies, and "Women in Africa and Her Diaspora: From Marginality to Empowerment," by 'Molara Ogundipe-Leslie. Bio-bibliographic notes on authors.

B12   **Braschi, Giannina (Puerto Rico).** *Empire of Dreams.* **Trans. Tess O'Dwyer. New Haven and London: Yale University Press, 1994. 220 pp.**

Short Fiction:
Assault on Time; Book of Clowns and Buffoons; Poems of the World; or, The Book of Wisdom; Pastoral; or, The Inquisition of Memories; Song of Nothingness; Epilogue; The Adventures of Mariquita Samper; The Life and Works of Berta Singerman; The Things That Happen to Men in New York!; The Queen of Beauty, Charm, and Coquetry; Gossip; Portrait of Giannina Braschi; Mariquita Samper's Childhood; The Raise; Manifesto on Poetic Eggs; The Building of the Waves of the Sea; Requiem for Solitude.

Includes an introduction by Alicia Ostriker and translator's note by Tess O'Dwyer.

B13   **Breton, Marcela, ed. and intro.** *Rhythm and Revolt: Tales of the Antilles.* **New York: Penguin, 1995. 278 pp.**

Short Stories:
Fanny Buitrago (Colombia), Caribbean Siren. **Lydia Cabrera** (Cuba), The Hill of Mambiala. **Magali García Ramis** (Puerto Rico), The Sign of Winter. **Ana Lydia Vega** (Puerto Rico), Cloud Cover Caribbean.

Includes brief bio-biographic notes on authors.

B14   **Busby, Margaret, ed. and intro.** *Daughters of Africa: An International Anthology of Words and Writings by Women of African Descent: From the Ancient Egyptian to the Present.* **New York: Pantheon Books, 1992. 1089 pp.**

Short Stories:
Carolina María de Jesús (Brazil), Diary: 1955 (excerpt from *Beyond all Pity*). **Aline França** (Brazil), excerpt from *A Mulher de Aleduma.* **Pilar López Gonzáles** (Cuba), It Was All Mamá's Fault.

Includes brief bio-bibliographic notes on authors, a bibliography of primary and secondary sources for authors as well as an extensive bibliography of further reading.

C1   Caistor, Nick, ed. and intro. *Columbus' Egg. New Latin American Stories on the Conquest.* Boston: Faber & Faber, 1992. 162 pp.

Short Stories:
Ana Valdés (Uruguay), The Peace of the Dead. **Luisa Valenzuela** (Argentina), Three Days. **Ana Lydia Vega** (Puerto Rico), Pateco's Little Prank.

C2   ___, ed. and intro. *The Faber Book of Contemporary Latin American Short Stories.* London: Faber & Faber, 1989. 188 pp.

Short Stories:
Isabel Allende (Chile), The Judge's Wife. **María Luisa Puga** (Mexico), The Trip. **Cristina Peri Rossi** (Uruguay), The Museum of Vain Endeavours. **Luisa Valenzuela** (Argentina), Up Among the Eagles.

Includes brief bio-bibliographic notes on authors.

C3   Campobello, Nellie (Mexico). *Cartucho* and *My Mother's Hands.* Trans. Doris Meyer and Irene Matthews. Austin: University of Texas Press, 1988. 129 pp.

Contents:
Cartucho: Men of the North; The Executed; Under Fire. *My Mother's Hands*: She Was; Once I Sought Her, Far Away Where She Lived a Life Shattered by Rifles' Ravages; Reader, Fill Your Heart with My Respect; She is Here; You and He; Her Love; Our Love; Her Skirt; Her God; The Men Left Their Mutilated Bodies Awaiting the Succor of These Simple Flowers; The Men of the Troop; The Dumb One; A Villa Man Like So Many Others; She and Her Machine; Jacinto's Deal; Plaza of the Lilacs; When We Came to a Capital City; A Letter for You.

Includes an introduction by Elena Poniatowska and translators' notes from both Meyer and Matthews. *Cartucho* is often called a novel, but consists of 56 sketches made up of autobiography, history, and poetry. *My Mother's Hands* is described as a poem by the translator. However, its format is that of short fictional pieces.

C4   Campos, Julieta (Mexico). *Celina or the Cats.* Trans. Leland Chambers and Kathleen Ross. Pittsburgh: Latin American Literary Review Press, 1995. 140 pp.

Short Fiction:
On Cats and Other Worlds; Celina or the Cats; The Baptism: All the Roses;

The House; The City.

Includes brief bio-bibliographic notes on the author and the translators.

C5   **Carlson, Lori M. and Cynthia L. Ventura, eds.** *Where Angels Glide at Dawn: New Stories from Latin America.* **New York: J.B. Lippincott, 1990. 114 pp.**

Short Stories:
Marjorie Agosín (Chile), A Huge Black Umbrella. **María Rosa Fort** (Peru), Tarma. **Barbara Mujica** (USA), Fairy Tale (originally written in English).

Includes an introduction by Isabel Allende, a glossary, and bio-bibliographic information on authors. Many of the stories are adaptations for young readers. Illustrations by José Ortega.

C6   **Carranza, Sylvia, and María Juana Cazabón, eds.** *Cuban Short Stories, 1959-1966.* **Havana: Book Institute, 1967. 229 pp.**

Short Stories:
Dora Alonso, The Rat. **María Elena Llano**, The Two of Us. **Ana María Simo**, Aunt Albertina's Last Party. **Evora Tamayo**, Sylvia.

Includes brief bio-bibliographic notes on contributors, a photograph of each author, and a Spanish/English glossary.

C7   **Cass, Canfield Jr., ed.** *Masterworks of Latin American Short Fiction: Eight Novellas.* **New York: Icon Editions, 1996. 385 pp.**

Short Fiction:
Ana Lydia Vega (Puerto Rico), Miss Florence's Trunk.

Includes an introduction by Ilan Stavans.

C8   **Castellanos, Rosario (Mexico).** *City of Kings.* **Trans. Robert S. Rudder and Gloria Chacón de Arjona. Pittsburgh: Latin American Literary Review Press, 1992. 143 pp.**

Short Stories:
Death of the Tiger; The Truce; Aceite guapo; The Luck of Teodoro Méndez Acúba; Modesta Gómez; Coming of the Eagle; The Fourth Vigil; The Wheel of Hunger; The Gift, Refused; Arthur Smith Finds Salvation.

Includes an introduction by Claudia Schaefer, bio-bibliographic notes on the author and editors, and a Spanish-English glossary.

C9   **Castro-Klarén, Sara, and Sylvia Molloy, eds.** *Women's Writing in Latin America: An Anthology.* **Boulder: Westview Press, 1991. 362 pp.**

Short Fiction:
Diamela Eltit (Chile), Luminated (excerpt from the novel *Lumpérica*). **Elena Garro** (Mexico), Before the Trojan War. **Lygia Fagundes Telles** (Brazil), The Sauna. **Norah Lange** (Argentina), Childhood Copybooks (excerpt from *Cuadernos de infancia*). **Clarice Lispector** (Brazil), Luminescence; Since One Has to Write (aphorisms and short prose). **Silvina Ocampo** (Argentina), The Basement; The Mortal Sin. **Victoria Ocampo** (Argentina), Emily Bronte; *Terra incognita* (excerpt from same); From Primer to Book (excerpt from *De la cartilla al libro*), The Archipelago (excerpt from *Archipiélago*), The Insular Empire (excerpt from *El imperio insular*). **Elvira Orphée** (Argentina), Silence; Do Not Mistake Eternities; Voices That Grew Old. **Cristina Peri Rossi** (Uruguay), The Nature of Love. **Nélida Piñón** (Brazil), I Love My Husband.

Includes an extensive introduction by Sara Castro-Klarén, brief bio-bibliographic notes on authors, and primary and secondary bibliographies for each author.

C10   **Chávez-Vásquez, Gloria (Colombia).** *Opus Americanus: Short Stories.* **Trans. Gloria Chávez-Vásquez. White Owl Editions, 1993. 189 pp.**

Short Stories:
The Firefly and the Mirror (La luciérnaga y el espejo); The Termites (Las termitas); Sincronio, the Bird of Wonder (Sincronio, el ave fénix); The Subwaynauts (Diario de un subwaynauta); From La Alameda to New York (De La Alameda a Nueva York); A Broken Vase (Un búcaro roto); A Consulate's Tale (Un cuento de consulado); The Human Virus (El virus humano); The American Legend of the Creation of the Brain (La leyenda americana de la creación del cerebro); The Origins of Bureaucracy (Orígenes de la burocracia); The Lookout (El mirador); Sister Orfelina (Sor Orfelina).

Includes a brief introduction by Mario Sandoval. Bilingual edition.

C11   **Cheuse, Alan, and Caroline Marshall, eds.** *The Sound of Writing.* **New York: Anchor Books, 1991. 239 pp.**

Short Stories:
Rosario Ferré (Puerto Rico), The Dreamer's Portrait.

Includes a preface by Caroline Marshall and bio-bibliographic notes on authors.

C12   **Clerk, Jayana, and Ruth Siegel, eds. and preface.** *Modern Literatures of the Non-Western World. Where the Waters are Born.* **New York: HarperCollins College Division, 1995. 1223 pp.**

Short Stories:
Isabel Allende (Chile), Our Secret. **María Luisa Bombal** (Chile), Sky, Sea and Earth. **Rachel de Queiroz** (Brazil), Tangerine Girl. **Lygia Fagundes Telles** (Brazil), The Ants. **Rosario Ferré** (Puerto Rico), The Youngest Doll. **Silvina Ocampo** (Argentina), The Servant's Slaves. **Gabriela Mistral** (Chile), Song. **Nélida Piñón** (Brazil), Brief Flower. **Ana Lydia Vega** (Puerto Rico), ADJ, Inc.

The appendices include general bio-bibliographic references as well as alternate tables of contents by theme, country, and genre. Besides Latin American and Caribbean literature, this volume also includes literatures from Africa, the Middle East, East, South, and Southeast Asia, as well as aboriginal literatures from Australia and New Zealand. Each selection is followed by a set of questions titled "Discussion and Writing" and suggestions for "Research and Comparison." This volume is intended for use as a reader in university courses

C13   **Coelho Pinto, José Saldanha da Gama, ed.** *Contistas brasileiros. New Brazilian Short Stories.* **Trans. Rod W. Horton. Rio de Janeiro: Revista Branca, 1957. 238 pp.**

Short Stories:
Lygia Fagundes Telles, Happiness.

Includes very brief bio-bibliographic notes on authors. Bilingual edition.

C14   **Cohen, J.M., ed. and intro.** *Writers in the New Cuba: An Anthology.* **Harmondsworth & Baltimore: Penguin, 1967. 191 pp.**

Short Stories:
Ana María Simo, A Deathly Sameness; Growth of the Plant.

Includes bio-bibliographic notes on authors.

C15   Colchie, Thomas, ed. and intro. *A Hammock Beneath the Mangoes: Stories from Latin America.* New York: Penguin, 1994. 430 pp.

Short Stories:
Isabel Allende (Chile), Toad's Mouth. **Lygia Fagundes Telles** (Brazil), The Corset. **Rosario Ferré** (Puerto Rico), The Gift. **Clarice Lispector** (Brazil), Love. **Armonía Somers** (Uruguay), Waiting for Polidoro. **Ana Lydia Vega** (Puerto Rico), Story-Bound.

Includes bio-bibliographic notes on authors and editor.

C16   Correas de Zapata, Celia, ed. and intro. *Short Stories by Latin American Women: The Magic and the Real.* Houston: Arte Público Press, 1990. 224 pp.

Short Stories:
Isabel Allende (Chile), An Act of Vengeance. **Dora Alonso** (Cuba), Sophie and the Angel. **Helena Araujo** (Colombia), Asthmatic. **María Luisa Bombal** (Chile), The Tree. **Rosario Castellanos** (Mexico), Culinary Lesson. **Amparo Dávila** (Mexico), In Heaven; Shoes for the Rest of my Life. **Rima de Vallbona** (Costa Rica), Penelope's Silver Wedding Anniversary. **María Virginia Estenssoro** (Bolivia), The Child That Never Was. **Rosario Ferré** (Puerto Rico), The Poisoned Tale. **Elena Garro** (Mexico), Blame the Tlaxcaltecs. **Nora Glickman** (Argentina), The Last Emigrant. **Lucía Guerra** (Chile), The Virgin's Passion. **Liliana Heker** (Argentina), Berkeley or Mariana of the Universe. **Vlady Kociancich** (Argentina), Knight, Death and the Devil. **Luisa Mercedes Levinson** (Argentina), The Cove. **Clarice Lispector** (Brazil), Looking for Some Dignity. **María Elena Llano** (Cuba), In the Family. **Carmen Naranjo** (Costa Rica), Symbiotic Encounter. **Olga Orozco** (Argentina), The Midgets. **Antonia Palacios** (Venezuela), A Gentleman on the Train. **Cristina Peri Rossi** (Uruguay), Breaking the Speed Record. **Nélida Piñón** (Brazil), Big-bellied Cow. **Josefina Pla** (Paraguay), To Seize the Earth. **Elena Poniatowska** (Mexico), Park Cinema. **Teresa Porzecanski** (Uruguay), The Story of a Cat. **María Teresa Solari** (Peru), Death and Transfiguration of a Teacher. **Marta Traba** (Argentina), The Tale of the Velvet Pillows. **Luisa Valenzuela** (Argentina), Up Among the Eagles. **Ana Lydia Vega** (Puerto Rico), Caribbean. **Alicia Yánez Cossío** (Ecuador), The IWM 1000.

Includes a foreword by Isabel Allende and brief bio-bibliographical notes on the authors and translators.

C17   Coverdale Sumrall, Amber, ed. and preface. *Lover: Stories by Women.*

Freedom: The Crossing Press, 1992. 432 pp.

Short Stories:
Isabel Allende (Chile), Our Secret.

C18   Cranfill, Thomas Mabry, and George D. Schade, eds. *The Muse in Mexico: A Mid-century Miscellany.* Austin: University of Texas Press 1959. 179 pp.

Short Stories:
Guadalupe Amor, The Small Drawing Room. Guadalupe Dueñas, A Clinical Case.

Includes a brief preface by Thomas Mabry Cranfill.

D1   Dana, Doris. *Crickets and Frogs: A Fable.* Based on a Fable by Gabriela Mistral (Chile). New York: Atheneum, 1972. 28 pp.

Bilingual edition of a children's story.

D2   ___. *The Elephant and His Secret.* Based on a Fable by Gabriela Mistral (Chile). New York: Atheneum, 1974. 37 pp.

A children's story, side by side Spanish/English edition. Illustrations by Antonio Frasconi.

D3   de Onis, Harriet, ed., trans., and foreword. *The Golden Land. An Anthology of Latin American Folklore in Literature.* New York: Alfred A. Knopf, 1948. 395 pp.

Short Stories:
Carmen Lyra (Costa Rica), The Tales of My Aunt Panchita; Brer Rabbit, Businessman.

D4   de Vallbona, Rima (Costa Rica). *Flowering Inferno: Tales of Sinking Hearts.* Trans. Lillian Lorca de Tagle. Pittsburgh: Latin American Literary Review Press, 1994. 92 pp.

Short Stories:
The Word Weaver; The Secret Life of Grandma Anacleta; History's Editor; The Burden of Routine; Future Sorrows; The Peace Brigade; Hell; An Ephemeral Star; The Libel of Dismissal; Pythagoras' Illustrious Disciple; Intergalactic Crusade; Once More Cain and Abel; Confirmation of the Obvious; Distributive Justice.

D5 di Giovanni, Norman Thomas, and Susan Ashe, eds. and trans. *Celeste Goes Dancing and Other Stories: An Argentine Collection.* San Francisco: North Point Press, 1990. 184 pp.

Short Stories:
Estela dos Santos, Celeste Goes Dancing. **Liliana Heer**, The Letter to Ricardo. **Silvina Ocampo**, The Drawing Lesson.

Includes an introduction by Norman Thomas di Giovanni and bio-bibliographic notes on authors and editors.

D6 Donoso, José, and William A. Henkin, eds. *The TriQuarterly Anthology of Contemporary Latin American Literature.* New York: E.P. Dutton, 1969. 496 pp.

Short Stories:
Clarice Lispector (Brazil), excerpt from *The Apple in the Dark* (chapter four, part one).

Includes two introductory articles: "A Literature of Foundations" by Octavio Paz and "The New Latin American Novelists" by Rodríguez Monegal.

D7 Dowd, Siobhan, ed. and intro. **This Prison Where I Live: The PEN Anthology of Imprisioned Writers.** London: Cassell, 1993. 192 pp.

Short Stories:
Alicia Partnoy (Argentina), Rain; Ruth v. the Torturer.

Foreword by Joseph Brodsky.

E1 Erro-Peralta, Nora, and Caridad Silva-Núñez, eds. and intro. *Beyond the Border: A New Age in Latin American Women's Fiction.* Pittsburgh: Cleis Press, 1991. 223 pp.

Short Stories:
Isabel Allende (Chile), The Judge's Wife. **Lydia Cabrera** (Cuba), The Prize of Freedom. **Aída Cartagena Portalatín** (Dominican Republic), Donna Summer. **Rima de Vallbona** (Costa Rica), The Secret World of Grandmamma Anacleta. **Lygia Fagundes Telles** (Brazil), The Hunt. **Rosario Ferré** (Puerto Rico), Mercedes Benz 220 SL. **Lucía Fox** (Peru), The Wedding. **Elena Garro** (Mexico), Perfecto Luna. **Angélica Gorodischer** (Argentina), Under the Yubayas in Bloom. **Sylvia Lago** (Uruguay), Homelife. **Elena Poniatowska** (Mexico), Slide In, My Dark

One, Between the Crosstie and the Whistle. **Armonía Somers** (Uruguay), The Immigrant. **Gloria Stolk** (Venezuela), Crickets and Butterflies. **Luisa Valenzuela** (Argentina), Up Among the Eagles.

Includes primary and secondary bibliographies for each author and brief biographical notes. The appendix includes "The Short Story, Feminism and Latin American Women Writers: A Bibliography."

E2   **Esteves, Carmen C., and Lizabeth Paravisini-Gebert, eds. and intro. *Green Candy and Juicy Flotsam: Short Stories by Caribbean Women.* New Brunswick: Rutgers University Press, 1991. 273 pp.**

Short Stories:
Dora Alonso (Cuba), Cotton Candy. **Aída Cartagena Portalatín** (Domincan Republic), They Called Her Aurora (A Passion for Donna Summer). **Hilma Contreras** (Dominican Republic), Hair. **Rosario Ferré** (Puerto Rico), The Poisoned Story. **Magali García Ramis** (Puerto Rico), Cocuyo Flower. **Angela Hernández** (Dominican Republic), How to Gather the Shadows of the Flowers. **Olga Nolla** (Puerto Rico), No Dust Is Allowed in this House. **Ana Lydia Vega** (Puerto Rico), ADJ, Inc. **Mirta Yáñez** (Cuba), Of Natural Causes.

Includes bio-bibliographic notes and primary and secondary bibliographies for each author. Also includes stories by francophone and anglophone writers.

F1   **Fagundes Telles, Lygia (Brazil). *Tigrela and Other Stories.* Trans. Margaret A. Neves. New York: Avon Books, 1986. 152 pp.**

Short Stories:
The Ants; Rat Seminar; The Consultation; Yellow Nocturne; The Presence; The Touch on the Shoulder; The X in the Problem; Crescent Moon in Amsterdam; Lovelorn Dove (A Story of Romance); WM; The Sauna; Herbarium; Tigrela; Dear Editor.

Includes brief bio-bibliographic notes on the authors.

F2   **Fernández, Roberta, ed., preface, and intro. *In Other Words: Literature by Latinas of the United States.* Houston: Arte Público Press, 1994. 554 pp.**

Short Fiction:
Elena Castedo (Spain/Chile), excerpt from *Paradise*. **Nora Glickman** (Argentina), A Day in New York. **Aurora Levins Morales** (Puerto Rico),

A Remedy for Heartburn. **Bessy Reyna** (Cuba/Panama), And This Blue Surrounding Me Again.

Each selection is preceded by bio-bibliographic notes on the author and a photograph. Includes a foreword by Jean Franco, a selected bibliography of Latina literature of the United States, and brief bio-bibliographic notes on the translators and the critic (Jean Franco).

F3   **Fernández Olmos, Margarite, and Lizabeth Paravisini-Gebert, eds. and intro.** *Pleasure in the Word: Erotic Writing by Latin American Women.* **Fredonia: White Pine Press, 1994. 284 pp.**

Short Fiction:
Isabel Allende (Chile), excerpt from *The House of the Spirits.* **Albalucía Angel** (Colombia), excerpt from *The Spotted Bird Perched High Above Upon the Tall Green Lemon Tree...* **Pía Barros** (Chile), Foreshadowing of a Trace; A Smell of Wood and of Silence. **María Luisa Bombal** (Chile), excerpt from *The Last Mist.* **Matilde Daviú** (Venezuela), The Woman Who Tore Up the World. **Rosario Ferré** (Puerto Rico), Rice and Milk. **Beatriz Guido** (Argentina), excerpt from *The House of the Angel.* **Angela Hernández** (Dominican Republic), How to Gather the Shadows of the Flowers. **María Luisa Mendoza** (Mexico), excerpt from *Ausencia's Tale.* **Silvina Ocampo** (Argentina), Albino Orma. **Renata Pallotini** (Brazil); Woman Sitting on the Sand. **Cristina Peri Rossi** (Uruguay), The Witness; Ca Foscar. **Alejandra Pizarnik** (Argentina); Words, The Lady Buccaneer of Pernambuco or Hilda the Polygraph; The Bloody Countess. **Elena Poniatowska** (Mexico), Happiness. **Rosamaría Roffiel** (Mexico), excerpt from *Amora.* **Luisa Valenzuela** (Argentina), Dirty Words; excerpt from *The Efficacious Cat*: The Fucking Game. **Ana Lydia Vega** (Puerto Rico), Lyrics for a Salsa and Three Soneos by Request.

Includes brief preface by Marjorie Agosín, bio-bibliographic notes on editors and authors, and a bibliography of original works in Spanish and Portuguese.

F4   ___, eds. and intro. *Remaking a Lost Harmony: Stories from the Hispanic Caribbean.* **Fredonia: White Pine Press, 1995. 249 pp.**

Short Stories:
Aída Cartagena Portalatín (Dominican Republic), The Path to the Ministry. **Hilma Contreras** (Dominican Republic), Mambrú Did Not Go to War. **Soledad Cruz** (Cuba), Fritters and Moons. **Rosario Ferré** (Puerto Rico), This Noise Was Different. **Magali García Ramis** (Puerto Rico), Corinne, Amiable Girl. **Angela Hernández** (Dominican Republic),

Silvia. **Verónica López Kónina** (Russia-Cuba), How Do You Know, Vivian? **Mayra Montero** (Cuba), Under the Weeping Willow. **Olga Nolla** (Puerto Rico), Requiem for a Wreathless Corpse. **Ana Lydia Vega** (Puerto Rico), The Blind Buffalo. **Mirta Yáñez** (Cuba), Public Declaration of Love.

Includes a brief bio-bibliographic notes on editors, authors, translators, and cover artist.

F5   **Ferré, Rosario (Puerto Rico).** *Sweet Diamond Dust: A Novel and Three Stories of Life in Puerto Rico.* **Trans. Rosario Ferré. New York: Ballantine Books, 1988. 198 pp.**

Short Fiction:
Sweet Diamond Dust (novel); The Gift; Isolda's Mirror; Captain Candelario's Heroic Last Stand.

F6   ___. *The Youngest Doll.* **Trans. Rosario Ferré. Lincoln: University of Nebraska Press, 1991. 169 pp.**

Short Stories:
The Youngest Doll; The Poisoned Story; The Dust Garden; The Glass Box; The Fox Fur Coat; The Dreamer's Portrait; The House that Vanished; Amalia; Marina and the Lion; The Seed Necklace; The Other Side of Paradise; Sleeping Beauty; Mercedes Benz 220 SL; When Women Love Men; How I Wrote "When Women Love Men" (essay); On Destiny, Language, and Translation; or, Ophelia Adrift in the C. & O. Canal (essay).

Includes a foreword by Jean Franco and a bibliography of major works by Rosario Ferré.

F7   **Fremantle, Anne, ed. and preface.** *Latin American Literature Today.* **New York: New American Library, 1977. 342 pp.**

Short Stories:
Silvina Bullrich (Argentina), The Bridge. **Rosario Castellanos** (Mexico), excerpt from *Office of Tenebrae.* **Kitzia Hoffman** (Mexico), Old Adelina. **Clarice Lispector** (Brazil), The Man Who Appeared; Better Than to Burn. **Gabriela Mistral** (Chile), Castile (An Imaginary Encounter with Saint Theresa.

Includes brief bio-bibliographic notes on the authors.

G1   Geok-Lin Lim, Shirley, and Norman Spencer, eds. *One World of Literature.* Boston: Houghton Mifflin Co., 1993. 1182 pp.

Short Stories:
Isabel Allende (Chile), Phantom. **Rosario Castellanos** (Mexico), Death of the Tiger. **Rosario Ferré** (Puerto Rico), Mercedes Benz 220 SL. **Clarice Lispector** (Brazil), The Body. **Luisa Valenzuela** (Argentina), I'm Your Horse in the Night.

Includes a brief introduction to literature from every continent. The appendix includes bibliographies organized into general bibliographies and by country (critical studies).

G2   Gibbons, Reginald, ed. and intro. *New Writing from Mexico.* A special issue of *TriQuarterly* magazine. Evanston: TriQuarterly and Northwestern University, 1992. 420 pp.

Short Fiction:
Carmen Boullosa, Storms of Torment. **Barbara Jacobs**, The Time I Got Drunk. **Mónica Lavín**, The Lizard. **Mónica Mansour**, In Secret. **Angeles Mastretta**, excerpt from *Big-Eyed Women*. **Silvia Molina**, Starting Over. **María Luisa Puga**, The Natural Thing to Do. **Bernarda Solís**, Art and Monsters. **Gloria Velázquez**, Temptress of the Torch-Pines.

Includes brief bio-bibliographic notes on authors and translators.

G3   Goldberg, Isaac, ed. *Brazilian Tales.* Boston: Four Seas, 1921. 149 pp.

Short Stories:
Carmen Dolores, Aunt Zeze's Tears.

Includes preliminary remarks by Isaac Goldberg.

G4   Gómez, Alma, Cherrie Moraga, and Mariana Romo-Carmona, eds. and intro. *Cuentos: Stories by Latinas.* New York: Kitchen Table, Women of Color Press, 1983. 241 pp.

Short Stories:
María Carolina de Jesús (Brazil), Childhood. **Miriam Díaz-Diocaretz** (Chile), Juani en tres tiempos. **Cicera Fernándes de Oliveira** (Brazil), We Women Suffer More than Men. **Aurora Levins Morales** (Puerto Rico), El bacalao viene de más lejos y se come aquí. **Gloria Liberman** (Chile), La confesión. **Aleida Rodríguez** (Cuba), A Month in a Nutshell.

Mariana Romo-Carmona (Chile), La virgen en el desierto. **Sara Rosel** (Cuba), El viaje. **Lake Saris** (Chile), The March. **Luz María Umpierre** (Puerto Rico), La Veintiuna. **Iris Zavala** (Puerto Rico), Kiliagonia.

Includes a Spanish/English glossary.

G5   **Graziano, Frank, ed. and intro.** *Alejandra Pizarnik: A Profile.* **Durango: Logbridge-Rhodes, Inc., 1987. 143 pp.**

Short Prose:
Alejandra Pizarnik (Argentina), Nocturnal Singer; Fragments for Dominating Silence; Sorceries; Roads of the Mirror; A Dream Where Silence is Made of Gold; Extraction of the Stone of Folly; Night Shared in the Memory of an Escape; excerpts from *The Musical Hell*: Fundamental Stone; Desire of the Word; L'obscurité des eaux; The Word that Cures; Names and Figures; The Possessed Among Lilacs; excerpts from *Texts of Shadow and Last Poems:* Words; Small Poems in Prose; On Time and Not; The Understanding; Tangible Absence; A Mystical Betrayal; House of Favors; The Lady Buccaneer of Pernambuco or Hilda the Polygraph; The End; Portrait of Voices. Excerpts from *The Bloody Countess:* The Iron Virgin; The Mirror of Melancholy; Blood Bath; Severe Measures.

Includes notes on the author and a bibliography of her works.

G6   **Grossman, William L., ed., trans., and intro.** *Modern Brazilian Short Stories.* **Berkeley: University of California Press, 1967. 167 pp.**

Short Stories:
Rachel de Queiroz, Metonymy, or the Husband's Revenge. **Clarice Lispector**, The Crime of the Mathematics Professor. **Marília São Paulo Penna e Costa**, The Happiest Couple in the World. **Dinah Silveira de Queiroz**, Guidance.

Includes bio-bibliographic notes on authors.

H1   **Halperin, Daniel, ed. and intro.** *The Art of the Tale: An International Anthology of Short Stories 1945-1985.* **New York: Viking Penguin Books, 1986. 818 pp.**

Short Stories:
Luisa Valenzuela (Argentina), I'm Your Horse in the Night.

Includes bio-bibliographical notes on authors.

H2   Hanson, Ron, and Jim Shepard, eds. and intro. *You've Got to Read This: Contemporary American Writers Introduce Stories That Held Them in Awe.* New York: Harper Perennial, 1994. 630 pp.

Short Stories:
Clarice Lispector (Brazil), The Smallest Woman in the World.

Includes an introduction to the story written by Julia Alvarez.

H3   Hazelton, Hugh, and Gary Geddes, eds. and intro. *Compañeros: An Anthology of Writings about Latin America.* Ontario: Cormorant Books, 1990. 320 pp.

Short Stories:
Marilú Mallet (Chile), The Loyal Order of the Time-Clock.

Includes brief bio-bibliographic notes on authors.

H4   Heker, Liliana (Argentina). *The Stolen Party and Other Stories.* Trans. and afterword, Alberto Manguel. Toronto: Coach House Press, 1994. 136 pp.

Short Stories:
Georgina Requeni or the Chosen One; Early Beginnings or Ars Poética; Family Life; Bishop Berkeley or Mariana of the Universe; Jocasta; The Stolen Party.

These stories were taken from three of Heker's other collections: *Aquarius* (1972), *Resplandor que se apagó en el mundo* (1977), and *Peras del mal* (1982).

H5   Howe, Irving, and Ilana Wiener Howe, eds. *Short Stories. An Anthology of the Shortest Stories.* Boston: David R. Grodine Publisher, 1982. 262 pp.

Short Stories:
Luisa Valenzuela (Argentina), The Censors.

Includes an introduction by Irving Howe.

H6   Howes, Barbara, ed. and intro. *From the Green Antilles: Writings of the Caribbean.* New York: Macmillan, 1966. 368 pp.

Short Stories:
Lydia Cabrera (Cuba), Turtle's Horse; Walo-Wila.

Includes bio-bibliographic notes on authors. Also includes the work of English, French, and Dutch-speaking authors. A brief introduction precedes each language group.

H7   ___, ed. and intro. *The Eye of the Heart: Short Stories from Latin America.* New York: Avon Books, 1973. 576 pp.

Short Stories:
María Luisa Bombal (Chile), The Tree. **Clarice Lispector** (Brazil), The Smallest Woman in the World. **Gabriela Mistral** (Chile), Why Reeds are Hollow. **Dinah Silveira de Queiroz** (Brazil), Tarciso. **Armonía Somers** (Uruguay), Madness.

Includes bio-bibliographic notes on authors and translators.

I1   Ibieta, Gabriella, ed. and intro. *Latin American Writers: Thirty Stories.* New York: St. Martin's Press, 1993. 355 pp.

Short Stories:
María Luisa Bombal (Chile), New Islands. **Lydia Cabrera** (Cuba), The Hill Called Mambiala. **Rosario Castellanos** (Mexico), Cooking Lesson. **Rosario Ferré** (Puerto Rico), Sleeping Beauty. **Elena Garro** (Mexico), The Day We Were Dogs. **Clarice Lispector** (Brazil), The Imitation of the Rose; The Departure of the Train. **Cristina Peri Rossi** (Uruguay), The Influence of Edgar Allan Poe on the Poetry of Raimundo Arias. **Nélida Piñón** (Brazil), Adamastor. **Luisa Valenzuela** (Argentina), Strange Things Happen Here. **Alicia Yánez Cossío** (Ecuador), Sabotage.

Includes bio-bibliographic notes on authors.

J1   Jacobsen McLennan, Karen, ed. and intro. *Nature's Ban. Women's Incest Literature.* Boston: Northeastern University Press, 1996. 394 pp.

Short Stories:
Rosario Ferré (Puerto Rico), Amalia.

Includes brief bio-bibliographic notes on authors and a select bibliography consisting of: Literature by and about Selected Authors; Critical, Historical, and Clinical References (about incest); and Additional Literature about Incest: Fiction, Poetry, Memoir, and Drama.

J2   Jaffe, Harold, ed. *Fiction International 25. Special Issue: Mexican Fiction.* San Diego: San Diego State University Press, 1994. 277 pp.

Short Stories:
Luz Mercedes Barrera, Molding You. **Acela Bernal**, The Taste of Good Fortune. **Silvia Castillejos Peral**, Tomorrow the World Ends. **Ana Clavel**, Dark Tears of a Mere Sleeper. **Regina Cohen**, Jazzbluesing. **Hilda Rosina Conde Zambada**, Sonatina. **Josefina Estrada**, Women in Captivity. **Cristina Ibarra**, The Little Eastern Star. **Patricia Laurent Kullick**, Crazy Cuts. **Mónica Lavín**, Nicolasa's Lace. **Regina Swain**, The Devil Also Dances in the Aloha; Señorita Supermán and the Instant Soup Generation.

Includes an introduction by Gabriel Trujillo Muñoz, "Turn-of-the-Century Mexican Narrative: A Tourist Guide."

J3   Jaramillo, Enrique Levi, ed. and prologue. *When New Flowers Bloomed: Short Stories by Women Writers from Costa Rica and Panama.* Pittsburgh: Latin American Literary Review Press, 1991. 208 pp.

Short Stories:
Lilia Algandona (Panama), Nightmare at Deep River. **Giovanna Benedetti** (Panama), The Rain on the Fire; The Scent of Violets. **Rosa María Britton** (Panama), The Wreck of the Enid Rose. **Delfina Collado** (Costa Rica), Garabito the Indomitable; The Indian Mummy. **Rima de Vallbona** (Costa Rica), The Good Guys; The Wall. **Griselda López** (Panama), One Minute; I'll Eat the Land. **Carmen Lyra** (Costa Rica), Ramona, Woman of the Ember; Estefania. **Emilia Macaya** (Costa Rica), Alcestis; Eva. **Carmen Naranjo** (Costa Rica), My Byzantine Grandmother's Two Medieval Saints; When New Flowers Bloomed. **Eunice Odio** (Costa Rica), The Vestige of the Butterfly. **Yolanda Oreamuno** (Costa Rica), Urban Wake; Of Their Obscure Family. **Bertalicia Peralta** (Panama), Elio. **Julieta Pinto** (Costa Rica), The Country Schoolmaster; The Meeting. **Bessy Reyna** (Panama), And This Blue Surrounding Me Again. **Graciela Rojas Sucre** (Panama), Wings. **Isis Tejeira** (Panama), The Birth; The Piano of My Desire. **Victoria Urbano** (Costa Rica), Death in Mallorca.

Includes bio-bibliographic notes on authors, translators, and the editor. Also includes the bibliographies: "Studies on Literature from Costa Rica: A General Bibliography," "Studies on Literature from Panama: A General Bibliography," "Anthologies of (or including) Latin American Women Writers in English and Spanish," and "General Bibliographies of (or including) Latin American Women Writers."

J4   Jaramillo, Enrique, and Leland Chambers, eds. and intro.
Contemporary Short Stories from Central America. Austin: University
of Texas Press, 1994. 275 pp.

Short Stories:
Rosa María Britton (Panama), Love is Spelled with a "G." **Carmen
Naranjo** (Costa Rica), Floral Caper. **Bertalicia Peralta** (Panama), The
Village Virgin. **Julieta Pinto** (Costa Rica), Disobedience. **Victoria
Urbano** (Costa Rica), The Face.

Includes a bibliography for each country represented in the book and brief
bio-bibliographic notes on authors and translators.

J5   Jones, Earl, ed. *Selected Latin American Literature for Youth.* College
Station: Texas A & M University Press, 1968. 152 pp.

Short Stories:
Carmen Baez (Mexico), The Cylinder. **Carmen Lira** (Costa Rica),
Uvieta. **Elena Poniatowska** (Mexico), The Gift.

Includes brief bio-bibliographic notes on authors.

J6   Jones, Willis Knapp, ed. and intro. *Spanish American Literature in
Translation: A Selection of Prose, Poetry, and Drama Before 1888.
Volume I.* New York: Frederick Ungar, 1966. 356 pp.

Short Stories:
Clorinda Matto de Turner (Peru), Birds without Nests (excerpt from
Aves sin nido).

J7   ___, ed. and preface. *Spanish American Literature in Translation: A
Selection of Prose, Poetry, and Drama Since 1888. Volume II.* New
York: Frederick Ungar, 1963. 469 pp.

Short Stories:
Marta Brunet (Chile), Francina. **Carmen Lira** (Costa Rica), Uvieta.

Includes a lengthy introduction outlining the history of Latin American
literature since 1888.

K1   Kalechofsky, Robert, and Roberta Kalechofsky, eds. *Echad: An
Anthology of Latin American Jewish Writings.* Marblehead: Micah
Publications, 1980. 281 pp.

Short Stories:
Clarice Lispector (Brazil), Love; The Chicken. **Teresa Porzecanski** (Uruguay), Parricide. **Esther Seligson** (Mexico), A Wind of Dry Leaves; Luz de dos. **Alicia Steimberg** (Argentina), *Musicians and Watchmakers* (excerpt).

Includes a brief introduction by Roberta Kalechofsky and brief bio-bibliographic notes on authors and translators.

K2   ___, eds. *Echad 5: The Global Anthology of Jewish Women Writers.* Marblehead: Micah Publications, 1990. 426 pp.

Short Fiction:
Luisa Futoransky (Argentina), excerpt from the novel *Son cuentos chinos.* **Clarice Lispector** (Brazil), The Smallest Women in the World, The Daydreams of a Drunk Woman. **Teresa Porzecanski** (Uruguay), Dying of Love.

Includes an introduction by Roberta Kalechofsky and brief bio-bibliographic notes on authors.

K3   Katz, Naomi, and Nancy Milton, eds. and intro. *Fragment from a Lost Diary and Other Stories.* New York: Pantheon Books, 1973. 318 pp.

Short Stories:
Dora Alonso (Cuba), Times Gone By.

Includes bio-bibliographic information on authors and editors.

K4   Kerrigan, Anthony, ed. and foreword. *Extraordinary Tales.* New York: Herder and Herder, 1971. 144 pp.

Short Stories:
Delia Ingenieros (with Jorge Luís Borges) (Argentina), Odin. **Silvina Ocampo** (Argentina), The Inextinguishable Race.

Includes preliminary notes by Jorge Luís Borges and Adolfo Bioy Casares.

L1   Leonard, Kathy S., ed., trans., and intro. *Cruel Fictions, Cruel Realities: Short Stories by Latin American Women Writers.* Pittsburgh: Latin American Literary Press, 1997. 134 pp.

Short Fiction:
Gloria Artigas (Chile), Corners of Smoke. **Yolanda Bedregal** (Bolivia),

How Milinco Escaped from School; The Morgue (excerpt from the novel *Bajo el oscuro sol*). **Velia Calvimontes** (Bolivia), Coati 1950. **Nayla Chehade Durán** (Colombia), The Vigil; The Visit. **Silvia Diez Fierro** (Chile), The Sailor's Wife; We Must Keep Fanning the Master. **Inés Fernández Moreno** (Argentina), A Mother to be Assembled. **Gilda Holst** (Ecuador), The Competition. **María Eugenia Lorenzini** (Chile), Bus Stop #46. **Andrea Maturana** (Chile), Cradle Song; Out of Silence. **Viviana Mellet** (Peru), Good Night Air; The Other Mariana. **Ana María Shua** (Argentina), A Profession Like Any Other; Minor Surgery. **Mirta Toledo** (Argentina), The Hunchback; In Between.

Includes biographic information and a complete primary and secondary bibliography for each author. Foreword by Ana María Shua and notes on the editor/translator. Also includes a selected bibliography of anthologies in English containing short fiction by Latin American women writers.

L2   Levinson, Luisa Mercedes (Argentina). *The Two Siblings and Other Stories.* Trans. Sylvia Ehrlich Lipp. Pittsburgh: Latin American Literary Review, 1996. 157 pp.

Short Stories:
Sometime in Brussels; Penetrating a Dream; The Pale Rose of Soho; On the Other Side of the Shore; The Castle; The Girl with the Grey Woolen Gloves; The Two Siblings; Beyond the Grand Canyon; No Men for the Poncho Weavers; Ursula and the Hanged Man; Cobweb of Moons; The Islet; Fearful of Valparaíso; The Angel; The Minet; The Myth; With Passion...and Compassion; The Labyrinth of Time; A Singular Couple; The Boy; Residuum; The Other Shoes; The Cove.

Includes a prologue by Luisa Valenzuela and notes on the author and translator.

L3   Lewald, Ernest, ed., trans. and intro. *The Web: Stories by Argentine Women.* Washington, D.C.: Three Continents Press, 1983. 170 pp.

Short Stories:
Cecilia Absatz, A Ballet for Girls. **María Angélica Bosco**, Letter from Ana Karenina to Nora; Letter from Nora to Ana Karenina. **Silvina Bullrich**, The Lover; Self Denial. **Eugenia Calny**, Siesta. **Beatriz Guido**, Ten Times Around the Block; Takeover. **Amalia Jamilis**, Night Shift; Department Store. **Luisa Mercedes Levinson**, The Clearing; Mistress Frances. **Marta Lynch**, Bedside Story; Latin Lover. **Silvina Ocampo**, The Prayer. **Syria Poletti**, The Final Sin. **Reina Roffé**, Let's Hear What He Has to Say. **Luisa Valenzuela**, Change of Guard.

Includes bio-bibliographic notes on contributors and author photographs.

L4 **Lispector, Clarice (Brazil).** *Family Ties.* **Trans. and intro. Giovanni Pontiero. Austin: University of Texas Press, 1972. 156 pp.**

Short Stories:
The Daydreams of a Drunk Woman; Love; The Chicken; The Imitation of the Rose; Happy Birthday; The Smallest Woman in the World; The Dinner; Preciousness; Family Ties; Beginnings of a Fortune; Mystery in São Cristóvão; The Crime of the Mathematics Professor; The Buffalo.

L5 **___.** *The Foreign Legion: Stories and Chronicles.* **Trans. and afterword Giovanni Pontiero. Manchester: Carcanet, 1986. 219 pp.**

Short Stories:
The Misfortunes of Sofia; The Sharing of Bread; The Message; Monkeys; The Egg and the Chicken; Temptation; Journey to Petrópolis; The Solution; The Evolution of Myopia; The Fifth Story; A Sincere Friendship; The Obedient; The Foreign Legion.

Chronicles:
Includes arts criticism, character sketches, travel notes, conversations with her children, aphorisms, and personal reflections.

L6 **___.** *Soulstorm: Stories.* **Trans. and afterword Alexis Levitin. New York: New Directions Publications, 1989. 175 pp.**

Short Stories:
Explanation; Miss Algrave; The Body; The Way of the Cross; The Man Who Appeared; He Soaked Me Up; For the Time Being; Day by Day; Footsteps; A Complicated Case; Plaza Mauá; Pig Latin; Better Than to Burn; But it's Going to Rain; In Search of Dignity; The Departure of the Train; Dry Point of Horses; Where You Were at Night; A Report on a Thing; A Manifesto of the City; The Conjurations of Dona Frozina; That's Where I'm Going; The Dead Man in the Sea at Urea; Silence; An Emptying; A Full Afternoon; Such Gentleness; Waters of the Sea; Soulstorm; Life *au naturel*.

Includes an introduction by Grace Paley.

L7 **Luby, Barry J., and Wayne H. Finke, eds. and intro.** *Anthology of Contemporary Latin American Literature, 1960-1984.* **Rutherford: Fairleigh Dickinson University Press, 1986. 309 pp.**

Short Stories:
Magolo Cárdenas (Mexico), But What if I Liked the Panchos, Not the Beatles. **Aída Cartagena Portalatín** (Dominican Republic), Colita. **Matilde Daviú** (Venezuela), Ofelia's Transfiguration. **Margot Glantz** (Mexico), From *Genealogies* (excerpt).

Includes brief bio-bibliographic notes on authors.

M1   MacShane, Frank, and Lori M. Carlson, eds. *Return Trip Tango and Other Stories from Abroad.* New York: Columbia University Press, 1992. 255 pp.

Short Stories:
Cristina Peri Rossi (Uruguay), The Rebellious Sheep.

Includes an introduction by Anthony Burgess, "A Celebration of Translation," and brief bio-bibliographic notes on contributors.

M2   Maldonado, Clara Isabel (Bolivia). *Arcoiris de sueños (Retazos de una vida). Rainbow of Dreams (Patchwork of a Life).* Trans. Clara Isabel Maldonado. Sydney: Cervantes Publishing, 1993. 93 pp.

Short Stories:
21 Years.

Also includes poetry.

M3   Mallet, Marilú (Chile). *Voyage to the Other Extreme: Five Stories.* Trans. Alan Brown. Montreal: Vehicule, 1985. 105 pp.

Short Stories:
The Loyal Order of the Time-Clock; Blind Alley; Voyage to the Other Extreme; How Are You?; The Vietnamese Hats.

Includes brief bio-bibliographic notes on author and translator.

M4   Mancini, Pat McNees, ed. and intro. *Contemporary Latin American Short Stories.* New York: Ballantine Books, 1974. 479 pp.

Short Stories:
María Luisa Bombal (Chile), The Tree. **Clarice Lispector** (Brazil), The Imitation of the Rose.

Includes brief bibliography for further reading in English translation.

M5   Manguel, Alberto, ed. and foreword. *Black Water: Anthology of Fantastic Literature.* New York: Clarkson N. Potter Publishers, Inc., 1983. 967 pp.

       Short Stories:
       Silvina Ocampo (Argentina), The Friends.

       Includes bio-bibliographic notes on authors.

M6   ___, ed. and foreword. *Black Water 2: More Tales of the Fantastic.* New York: Clarkson N. Potter Publishers Inc., 1990. 941 pp.

       Short Stories:
       Isabel Allende (Chile), Two Words.

       Includes bio-bibliographic notes on authors.

M7   ___, ed. and intro. *Dark Arrows: Chronicles of Revenge.* New York: Penguin Books Ltd., 1985. 219 pp.

       Short Stories:
       Rachel de Queiroz (Brazil), Metonymy, or the Husband's Revenge.

       Includes brief bio-bibliographic notes on the authors and the editor.

M8   ___, ed. and intro. *Evening Games: Tales of Parents and Children.* New York: Clarkson N. Potter Publishers, Inc., 1987. 353 pp.

       Short Stories:
       Liliana Heker (Argentina), Jocasta.

       Includes bio-bibliographic notes on authors.

M9   ___, ed. and intro. *The Gates of Paradise: The Anthology of Erotic Short Fiction.* New York: Clarkson N. Potter Publishers, Inc., 1993. 689 pp.

       Short Stories:
       Isabel Allende (Chile), Wicked Girl. **Liliana Heker** (Argentina), Jocasta. **Elena Poniatowska** (Mexico), Park Cinema. **Armonía Somers** (Uruguay), The Fall.

       Includes bio-bibliographic notes on contributors.

M10   ___, ed. and intro. *Other Fires: Short Fiction by Latin American Women.* New York: Clarkson N. Potter Publishers, Inc., 1986. 222 pp.

Short Stories:
Albalucía Angel (Colombia), The Guerrillero. **Inés Arredondo** (Mexico), The Shunammite. **Lydia Cabrera** (Cuba), How the Monkey Lost the Fruit of His Labor. **Rosario Castellanos** (Mexico), Death of the Tiger. **Amparo Dávila** (Mexico), Haute Cuisine. **Rachel de Queiroz** (Brazil), Metonymy, or The Husband's Revenge. **Lygia Fagundes Telles** (Brazil), Tigrela. **Elena Garro** (Mexico), It's the Fault of the Tlaxcaltecas. **Angélica Gorodischer** (Argentina), Man's Dwelling Place. **Beatriz Guido** (Argentina), The Usurper. **Liliana Heker** (Argentina), The Stolen Party. **Vlady Kociancich** (Argentina), Knight, Death, and the Devil. **Clarice Lispector** (Brazil), The Imitation of the Rose. **Marta Lynch** (Argentina), Latin Lover. **Silvina Ocampo** (Argentina), Two Reports. **Alejandra Pizarnik** (Argentina), The Bloody Countess. **Elena Poniatowska** (Mexico), The Night Visitor. **Dinah Silveira de Queiroz** (Brazil), Guidance. **Armonía Somers** (Uruguay), The Fall.

Includes a foreword by Isabel Allende and bio-bibliographic notes on authors.

M11   ___, ed. and intro. *The Second Gates of Paradise: The Anthology of Erotic Short Fiction.* New York: Clarkson N. Potter Publishers, Inc., 1996. 692 pp.

Short Stories:
Alejandra Pizarnik (Argentina), The Bloody Countess.

Includes bio-bibliographic notes on contributors.

M12   ___, ed. and intro. *Soho Square III.* London: Bloomsbury Publishing Ltd., 1990. 287 pp.

Short Fiction:
Liliana Heker (Argentina), Early Beginnings or Ars Poética. **Amparo Dávila** (Mexico), Welcome to the Chelsea.

Includes extremely brief bio-bibliographical notes on authors.

M13   Menton, Seymour, ed. and preface. *The Spanish American Short Story: A Critical Anthology.* Berkeley: University of California Press, 1980. 496 pp.

Short Stories:
María Luisa Bombal (Chile), The Tree.

Includes brief bio-bibliographic notes on authors, a bibliography of anthologies of the Spanish-American short story (works in Spanish), and a bibliography of historical critical works.

M14   ___, ed. *Venezuelan Short Stories--Cuentos venezolanos.* Caracas: Monte Avila Editores, 1992. 275 pp.

Short Stories:
Laura Antillano, The Moon's Not a Piece of Cake (La luna no es pan de horno). **Teresa de la Parra**, The Story of Señorita Dust Grain, Ballerina of the Sun (Historia de la Señorita Grano de Polvo, bailarina del sol).

Includes a prologue by Lyda Aponte de Zacklin and brief bio-bibliographic notes on authors. Bilingual edition.

M15   Meyer, Doris, and Margarita Fernández Olmos, eds. and preface. *Contemporary Women Authors of Latin America: New Translations.* Brooklyn: Brooklyn College Press, 1983. 331 pp.

Short Stories:
Albalucía Angel (Colombia), Monguí. **Silvina Bullrich** (Argentina), The Divorce. **Lydia Cabrera** (Cuba), Obbara Lies But Doesn't Lie; The Hill Called Mambiala. **Rosario Castellanos** (Mexico), Cooking Lesson. **Amparo Dávila** (Mexico), Behind Bars. **Rosario Ferré** (Puerto Rico), When Women Love Men. **Elena Garro** (Mexico), The Day We Were Dogs. **Luisa Mercedes Levinson** (Argentina), The Myth. **Marta Lynch** (Argentina), Hotel Taormina. **Inés Malinow** (Argentina), Fixed Distance. **Angelina Muñiz** (Mexico), Rising, Mournful from the Earth. **Silvina Ocampo** (Argentina), The Mastiffs of Hadrian's Temple; Ana Valerga. **Victoria Ocampo** (Argentina), Misfortunes of an Autodidact. **Cristina Peri Rossi** (Uruguay), The Influence of Edgar Allan Poe on the Poetry of Raimundo Arias. **Nélida Piñón** (Brazil), Adamastor. **Tita Valencia** (Mexico), Video: Zoom in to Close-up; Zoom Back: Visions of Taking Flight. **Luisa Valenzuela** (Argentina), Generous Impediments Float Down the River. **Alicia Yánez Cossío** (Ecuador), Sabotage.

Includes bio-bibliographic notes on editors and translators and a selected bibliography.

M16   Milligan, Bryce, Mary Guerrero Milligan, and Angela de Hoyos, eds. and intro. *Daughters of the Fifth Sun: A Collection of Latina Fiction* *and Poetry*. New York: Riverhead Books, 1995. 284 pp.

Short Stories in Translation:
Marjorie Agosín (Chile), Adelina. **Rosario Ferré** (Puerto Rico), The Glass Box. **Mireya Robles** (Cuba), In the Other Half of Time.

Short Stories by Latina Authors Originally Written in English:Julia Alvarez (Dominican Republic), The Kiss. **Margarita Engle** (Cuba), Uncle Teo's Shorthand Cookbook. **Judith Ortiz Cofer** (Puerto Rico), Nada.

Includes a foreword by María Hinojosa and bio-bibliographic notes on authors. This collection includes Latin American, Latina, and Chicana writers.

M17   Moore, Evelyn, ed. and intro. *Sancocho: Stories and Sketches of Panama.* Panama: Panama American Publishing Co., 1938. 194 pp.

Short Stories:
Elda L. C. de Crespo, Village Fiesta; Maruja; Seña Paula. **Graciela Rojas Sucre**, On Account of the Piñata (excerpt from *Terruñadas de lo chico)*.

Includes bio-bibliographic notes on authors.

M18   Mordecai, Pamela, and Betty Wilson, eds. and intro. *Her True-True Name: An Anthology of Women's Writing from the Caribbean.* Oxford: Heinemann, 1989. 202 pp.

Short Stories:
Omega Agüero (Cuba), A Man, a Woman (excerpt from *El muro de medio metro)*. **Hilma Contreras** (Dominican Republic), The Window. **Rosario Ferré** (Puerto Rico), The Youngest Doll. **Magali García Ramis** (Puerto Rico), Every Sunday. **Carmen Lugo Filippi** (Puerto Rico), Recipes for the Gullible. **Ana Lydia Vega** (Puerto Rico), Cloud Cover Caribbean. **Mirta Yáñez** (Cuba), We Blacks All Drink Coffee.

Includes bio-bibliographic notes on authors. Also includes Anglophone and Francophone authors from the Caribbean.

M19   Muller, Gilberth, and John A. Williams, eds. and preface. *Bridges: Literature Across Cultures.* New York: McGraw Hill, Inc., 1994. 1048 pp.

Short Stories:
Luisa Valenzuela (Argentina), The Censors.

Includes bio-bibliographic notes on authors. This is a text suited for use in composition and introductory literature courses.

M20 **Muñiz-Huberman, Angelina (France/Mexico).** *Enclosed Garden.* **Trans. and preface Lois Parkinson Zamora. Pittsburgh: Latin American Literary Review Press, 1988. 103 pp.**

Short Stories:
On the Unicorn; In the Name of His Name; The Sarcasm of God; The Most Precious Offering; The Grand Duchess; Jocasta's Confession; Tlamapa; Salicio and Amarylis; Rising, Mournful, from the Earth; Gentlemen; The Fortunes of the Infante Arnaldos; The Minstrel; The Prisoner; Brief World; The Dream Curtain; Enclosed Garden; Longing; Vaguely, at Five in the Afternoon; Life Has No Plot; The Chrysalis of Clay Will Give Birth to a Butterfly; Retrospection.

Includes an afterword by Elena Poniatowska, "Meditation on the Enclosed Garden of Exile: A Conversation with Angelina Muñiz-Huberman."

N1 **Naranjo, Carmen (Costa Rica).** *There Never Was a Once Upon a Time.* **Trans. and foreword Linda Britt. Pittsburgh: Latin American Literary Review Press, 1989. 94 pp.**

Short Stories:
There Never Was a Once Upon a Time; Eighteen Ways to Make a Square; It Happened One Day; The Game That is Only Played Once; Everybody Loves Clowns; Maybe the Clock Played with Time; When I Invented Butterflies; Old Cat Meets Young Cat; Tell Me a Story, Olo.

O1 **Ocampo, Silvina (Argentina).** *Leopoldina's Dream.* **Trans. Daniel Balderston. London and New York: Penguin, 1988. 205 pp.**

Short Stories:
Thus Were Their Faces; Lovers; Revelation; The Fury; The Photographs; The Clock House; Mimoso; The Velvet Dress; The Objects; The Bed; The Perfect Crime; Azabache; Friends; The House of Sugar; Visions; The Wedding; Voice on the Telephone; Icera; The Autobiography of Irene; The Sibyl; Report on Heaven and Hell; The Mortal Sin; The Expiation; Livio Roca; The Doll; The Punishment; The Basement; The Guests; Carl Herst; Magush; The Prayer; Leopoldina's Dream.

Includes a brief preface by Jorge Luís Borges and an introduction by the author. Contains thirty-two short stories chosen from four of Ocampo's books: *Autobiografía de Irene, La furia y otros cuentos, Las imitadas*, and *Los días de la noche.* Includes brief bio-bibliographic notes on author and translator.

O2   O'hara, Maricarmen (Bolivia). *Cuentos para todos/Tales for Everybody.* Trans. Maricarmen O'hara. Ventura: Alegría Hispana Publications, 1994. 176 pp.

Short Stories:
He and She; A Simple Story; Mr. Turista's Breakfast; Little Joe Sticks; Olga's Diet; Mr. Slowly Slow; The Student Prince; A Man and a Woman; The Old Peasant; The Stronger; The 'Screaming Bag'; The Diamond; International Buffet; Questions and Answers; Truth; Hunger Strike; The Moon's Husband; Heddy the Airhead; The Peacock's Voice; The King's Peaches; The Smuggler; The Miser's Money; Marcelino's Job; The Divine Language; Pay Me!; The Grasshopper; The Bet; The House that Jack Built; Wooden Spoon; The Two Kings.

Bilingual edition. These stories are intended to be used to teach Spanish to English speakers. Each story is accompanied by a list of Spanish/English vocabulary.

P1   Paretsky, Sara, ed. and intro. *Women on the Case.* New York: Delacorte Press, 1996. 367 pp.

Short Stories:
Myriam Laurini (Argentina), Lost Dreams.

A volume of short fiction by women crime writers.

P2   Partnoy, Alicia (Argentina). *The Little School: Tales of Disappearance and Survival in Argentina.* Trans. Alicia Partnoy with Lois Athey and Sandra Braunstein. San Francisco: Cleis Press, 1986. 136 pp.

Short Stories:
The One-flower Slippers; Latrine; Birthday; My Names; Benja's First Night; Telepathy; Graciela; Around the Table; My Nose; Religion; A Conversation Under the Rain; A Puzzle; Tootbrush; Bread; The Small Box of Matches; Ruth's Father; Form of Address; Poetry; The Denim Jacket; A Beauty Treatment; Nativity.

Includes a brief preface by Bernice Johnson Reagon, introduction by Alicia

Partnoy, and bio-bibliographic notes on the author. Appendices include "Cases of the Disappeared at the Little School" and "Descriptions of the Guards at the Little School."

P3 ___, ed. *You Can't Drown the Fire: Latin American Women Writing in Exile.* San Francisco: Cleis Press, 1988. 258 pp.

Short Stories:
Marjorie Agosín (Chile), The Blue Teacups. **Alicia Dujovne Ortiz** (Argentina), Courage or Cowardice? **Cristina Peri Rossi** (Uruguay), The Influence of Edgar A. Poe on the Poetry of Raimundo Arias. **Marta Traba** (Argentina), The Day Flora Died. **Luisa Valenzuela** (Argentina), On the Way to the Ministry.

Includes notes on contributors.

P4 **Paschke, Barbara, and Davis Volpendesta, eds.** *Clamor of Innocence: Central American Short Stories.* San Francisco: City Lights Books, 1988. 174 pp.

Short Stories:
Rima de Vallbona (Costa Rica), Penelope on Her Silver Wedding Anniversary. **Carmen Lyra** (Costa Rica), Estefanía. **Carmen Naranjo** (Costa Rica), Walls. **Bertalicia Peralta** (Panama), The Guayacan Tree. **Bessy Reyna** (Panama), The Clean Ashtrays.

Includes brief bio-bibliographic notes on authors and translators.

P5 **Penelope Julia, and Sarah Valentine, eds.** *International Feminist Fiction.* Freedom: The Crossing Press, 1992. 333 pp.

Short Stories:
Rosario Ferré (Puerto Rico), The Youngest Doll. **Bertalicia Peralta** (Panama), A March Guayacán.

Includes brief notes on contributors and a brief introduction by Valerie Miner.

P6 **Pereira, Teresinka (Brazil).** *Help, I'm Drowning.* Trans. Angela de Hoyos. Chicago: Palos Heights Press, 1975. 18 pp.

Short Stories:
The Train and the Flowers; Solitude; Little Man.

Includes bio-bibliographic notes on the author and translator.

P7   **Peri Rossi, Cristina (Uruguay).** *A Forbidden Passion.* **Trans. Mary Jane Treacy. San Francisco: Cleis Press, 1993. 148 pp.**

          Short Stories:
          The Fallen Angel; A Forbidden Passion; The Bridge; Atlas; Guilt; The Trip; Patriotism; Gratitude Is Insatiable; The Nature of Love; The Parable of Desire; The Revelation; Final Judgement; A Moral Lesson; The Threshold; The Art of Loss; A Useless Passion; The Mirror Maker; The Bell Ringer; The Sentence; Singing in the Desert.

          Includes a brief introduction by Cristina Peri Rossi and bio-bibliographic notes on the author and translator.

P8   **Picon Garfield, Evelyn, ed. and intro.** *Women's Fiction from Latin America: Selections from Twelve Contemporary Authors.* **Detroit: Wayne State University Press, 1988. 355 pp.**

          Short Fiction
          Isabel Allende (Chile), Rosa the Beautiful (excerpt from *The House of the Spirits*). **Lydia Cabrera** (Cuba), The Mire of Almendares; Tatabisako. **Julieta Campos** (Cuba/Mexico), *A Redhead Named Sabina* (excerpts from the novel); All the Roses. **Elena Garro** (Mexico), The Tree. **Clarice Lispector** (Brazil), Love; Family Ties. **Carmen Naranjo** (Costa Rica), Ondina; Why Kill the Countess? **Elvira Orphée** (Argentina), Angel's Last Conquest (excerpt from the novel); The Silken Whale. **Nélida Piñón** (Brazil), Bird of Paradise; The New Kingdom. **Armonía Somers** (Uruguay), The Tunnel; The Burial; Plunder. **Marta Traba** (Argentina), *Mothers and Shadows* (excerpt from the novel); Conformity; All in a Lifetime. **Luisa Valenzuela** (Argentina), Blue Water Man; Other Weapons; I'm Your Horse in the Night.

          Includes bio-bibliographic notes, a photograph, and a primary and secondary bibliography for each author.

P9   **Poey, Delia, ed. and intro.** *Out of the Mirrored Garden: New Fiction by Latin American Women.* **New York: Anchor Books, 1996. 222 pp.**

          Short Stories:
          Carmen Boullosa (Mexico), So Disappear. **Rosa María Britton** (Panama), Death Lies on the Cots. **Julieta Campos** (Mexico), Allegories. **Elena Castedo** (Spain/Chile), Ice Cream. **Marta Cerda** (Mexico), A Time of Mourning. **Diamela Eltit** (Chile), Even if I Bathed in the Purest

Waters. **Rosario Ferré** (Puerto Rico), Amalia. **Magali García Ramis** (Puerto Rico), A Script for Every House. **Angela Hernández** (Dominican Republic), Teresa Irene. **Barbara Jacobs** (Mexico), Aunt Luisita. **Vlady Kociancich** (Argentina), A Family Man. **Alcina Lubitch Domecq** (Guatemala), Bottles. **Angeles Mastretta** (Mexico), Aunt Elvira. **Carmen Naranjo** (Costa Rica), Over and Over. **Cristina Peri Rossi** (Uruguay), The Annunciation. **Elena Poniatowska** (Mexico), The Rupture. **Mirta Yáñez** (Cuba), Go Figure.

Includes bio-bibliographic notes on the authors and the editor, a brief selected bibliography of related anthologies, and a bibliography of authors' work in translation.

P10   Poletti, Syria (Argentina). *The King Who Forbade Balloons.* Trans. Norman Thomas di Giovanni and Susan Ashe. Buenos Aires: Ediciones de Arte Gaglianone, 1987. 33 pp.

A children's story.

P11   *Prize Stories from Latin America: Winner of the "Life en español" Literary Contest.* Garden City: Doubleday, 1963. 398 pp.

Short Stories:
Laura del Castillo (Argentina), A Plum for Coco.

Inclues a brief preface by Arturo Uslar Pietro and brief bio-bibliographic notes on authors.

R1   Ramírez, Anthony, ed. and trans. *The Best of Latin American Short Stories. Los mejores cuentos hispanoamericanos.* Los Angeles: Bilingual Book Press, 1994. 114 pp.

Short Stories:
María Silva Ossa (Chile). The Ship from Far Away (El barco de más allá).

Side by side Spanish-English bilingual edition. Includes a brief introduction, bio-bibliographic notes on authors, and a Spanish-English glossary.

R2   Ras, Barbara, ed. and preface. *Costa Rica: A Traveler's Literary Companion.* San Francisco: Whereabouts Press, 1994. 238 pp.

Short Stories:
Rima de Vallbona, The Chumico Tree; Mystery Stone. **Carmen Lyra,** Pastor's Ten Little Old Men. **Carmen Naranjo,** Believe it or Not; When New Flowers Bloomed. **Yolanda Oreamuno,** The Lizard with the White Belly; The Spirit of My Land. **Julieta Pinto,** The Blue Fish.

Includes a foreword by Oscar Arias, brief bio-bibliographic notes on authors and translators, and a glossary of Spanish terms.

R3   Reyes, Sandra, ed., intro., and trans. *One More Stripe to the Tiger: A Selection of Contemporary Chilean Poetry and Fiction.* Fayetteville: University of Arkansas Press, 1989. 311 pp.

Short Stories:
Cecilia Casanova, The Unmarriage. **Marta Blanco,** Sweet Companion.

Includes brief bio-biographical notes on authors.

R4   Rieder, Inés, ed. and preface. *Cosmopolis: Urban Stories by Women.* Pittsburgh: Cleis Press, 1990. 196 pp.

Short Stories:
Silvia Fanaro (Brazil), The Day I Met Miss America. **Berta Hiriart** (Mexico), Maestra Arellano.

Includes brief bio-bibliographic notes on authors.

R5   Rodríguez Monegal, Emir, and Thomas Colchie, eds. and intro. *The Borzoi Anthology of Latin American Literature.* Vol. 1 & 2. New York: Knopf, 1977. 982 pp.

Short Stories in Volume 2:
Clarice Lispector (Brazil), The Passion According to G.H.; **Nélida Piñón** (Brazil), House of Passion.

Volume 1 does not contain any short stories by Latin American women.

R6   Ross, Kathleen, and Yvette Miller, eds. *Scents of Wood and Silence: Short Stories by Latin American Women Writers.* Pittsburgh: Latin American Literary Review Press, 1991. 218 pp.

Short Stories:
Margarita Aguirre (Chile), The Black Sheep. **Claribel Alegría** (El Salvador), The Awakening. **Isabel Allende** (Chile), Tosca. **Albalucía**

Angel (Colombia), Down the Tropical Path. **Pía Barros** (Chile), Scents of Wood and Silence. **Lydia Cabrera** (Cuba), Susundamba Does Not Show Herself by Day. **Julieta Campos** (Mexico), The House. **Ana María del Río** (Chile), Wash Water. **Lygia Fagundes** Telles (Brazil), The Structure of the Soap Bubble. **Angélica Gorodischer** (Argentina), Camera Obscura. **Matilde Herrera** (Argentina), Eduardito Doesn't Like the Police. **Clarice Lispector** (Brazil), Beauty and the Beast, or, The Wound Too Great. **Silvia Molina** (Argentina), Autumn. **Sylvia Molloy** (Argentina), Sometimes in Illyria. **Carmen Naranjo** (Costa Rica), A Woman at Dawn. **Olga Nolla** (Puerto Rico), A Tender Heart. **Silvina Ocampo** (Argentina), Creation (An Autobiographical Story). **Cristina Peri Rossi** (Uruguay), The Art of Loss. **Nélida Piñón** (Brazil), The Heat of Things. **María Luisa Puga** (Mexico), Memories on the Oblique. **Mariella Sala** (Peru), From Exile. **Luisa Valenzuela** (Argentina), Tango. **Ana Lydia Vega** (Puerto Rico), Death's Pure Fire.

Includes an introduction by Kathleen Ross and bio-bibliographic notes on authors and translators. Appendices include primary and secondary bibliographies for each author and bibliographies: "General Works on Women Writers and Feminist Literary Criticism," "Works on Latin American Women," "Anthologies of (or including) Latin American Women Writers in English and Spanish," and "General Bibliographies of (or including) Latin American Women Writers."

R7   Rowe, L. S., and Pedro de Alba, eds. *The Literature of Latin America. Volume I of the Series on Literature-Art-Music.* Washington, D.C.: Pan American Union, 1944. 64 pp.

Short Stories:
Teresa de la Parra (Venezuela), Mama Blanca. **Gabriela Mistral** (Chile), The Enemy.

S1   Sadlier, Darlene J., ed., trans., and intro. *One Hundred Years After Tomorrow: Brazilian Women's Fiction in the 20th Century.* Bloomington: Indiana University Press, 1992. 241 pp.

Short Fiction:
Lúcia Benedetti, My Uncle Ricardo. **Emi Bulhões Carvalho da Fonseca**, In the Silence of the Big House. **Marina Colasanti**, Little Girl in Red, on Her Way to the Moon. **Lia Correia Dutra**, A Perfect World. **Sonia Coutinho**, Every Lana Turner Has Her Johnny Stompanato. **Rachel de Queiroz**, excerpt from *The Year Fifteen*. **Márcia Denser**, The Vampire of Whitehouse Lane. **Carmen Dolores**, A Drama in the Countryside. **Sra. Leando Dupré**, excerpt from *We Were Six*. **Lygia Fagundes Telles**, Just

a Saxophone. **Hilda Hilst**, Agda. **Tania Jamardo Faillace**, Dorceli. **Clarice Lispector**, The Flight. **Elisa Lispector**, The Fragile Balance. **Júlia Lopes de Almeida**, excerpt from *He and She*. **Lya Luft**, excerpt from *The Left Wing of the Angel*. **Adalgisa Nery**, Premeditated Coincidence. **Nélida Piñón**, Near East. **Dinah Silveira de Queiroz**, Jovita. **Edla Van Steen**, The Sleeping Beauty (Script of a Useless Life).

Includes bio-bibliographic notes on authors.

S2   Salmonson, Jessica Amanda, ed. and preface. *What Did Miss Darrington See?: An Anthology of Feminist Supernatural Fiction.* New York: The Feminist Press, 1989. 263 pp.

Short Stories:
Armonía Somers (Uruguay), The Fall. **Luisa Valenzuela** (Argentina), The Teacher.

Includes an introduction by Rosemary Jackson, bio-bibliographic notes on authors, and a bibliography of recommended reading of women's fiction.

S3   Santiago, Roberto, ed., intro. *Boricuas: Influential Puerto Rican Writings--An Anthology.* New York: One World Ballantine Books, 1995. 355 pp.

Short Stories:
Ana Lydia Vega, Aerobics for Love.

Includes short stories by other Puerto Rican women writers (Nicholasa Mohr, Judith Ortiz Cofer, Esmeralda Santiago) which were originally written in English. Also includes poetry and essays by some forty Puerto Rican authors, male and female.

S4   Santos, Rosario, ed. *And We Sold the Rain: Contemporary Fiction from Central America.* New York: Four Walls Eight Windows, 1988. 215 pp.

Short Stories:
Claribel Alegría (El Salvador), Boardinghouse. **Jacinta Escudos** (El Salvador), Look at Lislique, See How Pretty It Is. **Carmen Naranjo** (Costa Rica), And We Sold the Rain. **Bertalicia Peralta** (Panama), A March Guayacán.

Includes an introduction by Jo Anne Engelbert and brief bio-bibliographic notes on authors and translators.

S5   Schulte, Rainer, ed. "International Short Fiction." *Mundus Artium* 8.2 (1975). 156 pp.

Short Stories:
Luisa Valenzuela (Argentina), The Door.

Includes a foreword by Lucia Getsi and bio-bibliographical notes on contributors.

S6   ___. "International Women's Issue." *Mundus Artium* 7.2 (1974). 160 pp.

Short Stories:
Concepción T. Alzola (Cuba), Don Pascual Was Buried Alone.

S7   Schulte, Rainer, et al., eds. "Special Latin American Fiction Issue." *Mundus Artium* 3.3 (1970). 124 pp.

Short Stories:
Vlady Kociancich (Argentina), False Limits. **Nélida Piñón** (Brazil), Big-bellied Cow.

Includes bio-bibliographic notes on contributors.

S8   **Shapard, Robert, and James Thomas, eds.** *Sudden Fiction: 60 Short-Short Stories.* **New York: W.W. Norton and Co., Inc., 1989. 342 pp.**

Short Stories:
Clarice Lispector (Brazil), The Fifth Story. **Luisa Valenzuela** (Argentina), The Verb *To Kill*. **Edla Van Steen** (Brazil), Mr. and Mrs. Martins.

Includes an introduction by Charles Baxter.

S9   **Smorkaloff, Pamela María, ed. and intro.** *If I Could Write This in Fire: An Anthology of Literature from the Caribbean.* **New York: New Press, 1994. 374 pp.**

Short Stories:
Chely Lima (Cuba), Monologue with Rain; Common Stories. **Ana Lydia Vega** (Puerto Rico), The Day It All Happened; Port-au-Prince; Below.

Includes a selected bibliography of prose works by the authors included in the volume.

S10   Solomon, Barbara, ed. and intro. *Other Voices, Other Vistas. Short Stories from Africa, China, India, Japan, and Latin America.* New York: Penguin USA, 1992. 478 pp.

        Short Stories:
        Isabel Allende (Chile), Clarisa. **Luisa Valenzuela** (Argentina), Papito's Story.

        Includes bio-bibliographic notes on authors and a bibliography of selected Latin American anthologies in English.

S11   Stavans, Ilan, ed. and intro. *Tropical Synagogues: Short Stories by Jewish-Latin American Writers.* New York: Holmes & Meier, 1994. 239 pp.

        Short Stories:
        Aída Bortnik (Argentina), Celeste's Heart. **Margo Glantz** (Mexico), Genealogies. **Elisa Lerner** (Venezuela), Papa's Friends. **Clarice Lispector** (Brazil), Love. **Alcina Lubitch Domecq** (Guatemala), Bottles. **Angelina Muñiz-Huberman** (Mexico), In the Name of His Name. **Esther Seligson** (Mexico), The Invisible Hour. **Alicia Steimberg** (Argentina), Cecilia's Last Will and Testament.

        Includes bio-bibliographic notes and a primary and secondary bibliography for each author.

T1   Thomas, James, Denise Thomas, and Tom Hazuka, eds. *Flash Fiction. 72 Very Short Stories.* New York: W.W. Norton & Company, 1992. 224 pp.

        Short Stories:
        Luisa Valenzuela (Argentina), Vision Out of the Corner of One Eye.

        Brief introduction by James Thomas.

T2   Thomas, Sue, ed. and preface. *Wild Women: Contemporary Short Stories by Women Celebrating Women.* Woodstock: The Overlook Press, 1994. 368 pp.

        Short Stories:
        Isabel Allende (Chile), Two Words.

        Includes an introduction by Clarissa Pinkola Estés and bio-bibliographic notes on the authors.

T3   Torres-Rioseco, Arturo, ed. and intro. *Short Stories of Latin America.*
New York: Las Americas, 1963. 203 pp.

Short Stories:
María Luisa Bombal (Chile), The Tree. Guadalupe Dueñas (Mexico),
The Moribund.

Includes brief bio-bibliographic notes on authors.

T4   Troupe, Quincy, and Rainer Schulte, eds. and intro. *Giant Talk: An
Anthology of Third World Writings.* New York: Random House, 1975.
547 pp.

Short Stories:
Vlady Kociancich (Argentina), False Limits.

Includes brief bio-bibliographic notes on authors and editors and an
extensive bibliography divided into the following categories: African-
American and Puerto Rican-American Anthologies, African-American
Literary Criticism, Anthologies of African Poetry and Prose, Critical
Books of Essays on African Literature, Latin American Anthologies, and,
Periodicals, Journals, and Magazines.

U1   Urbano, Victoria, ed. *Five Women Writers of Costa Rica: Short Stories
by Carmen Naranjo, Eunice Odio, Yolanda Oreamuno, Victoria Urbano,
and Rima de Vallbona.* Beaumont: Asociación de Literatura Femenina
Hispánica, 1978. 131 pp.

Short Stories:
Rima de Vallbona, Chumico Tree; Penelope's Silver Wedding
Anniversary; Parable of the Impossible Eden. Carmen Naranjo, The
Flowery Trick; The Journey and the Journeys; Inventory of a Recluse.
Eunice Odio, Once There Was a Man; The Trace of the Butterfly.
Yolanda Oreamuno, High Valley; The Tide Returns at Night. Victoria
Urbano, Avery Island; Triptych.

Includes bio-bibliographic notes on contributors and a critical commentary
on the authors and their works.

V1   Valenzuela, Luisa (Argentina). *The Censors.* Trans. Hortense
Carpentier. Willimantic: Curbstone Press, 1992. 255 pp.

Short Stories:
The Best Shod (Los mejor calzados); The Snow White Watchman (El custodio blancanieves); The Censors (Los censores); Redtown Chronicles (Crónicas de pueblorrojo); Void and Vacuum (Vacío era el de antes); Papito's Story (La historia de Papito); Country Carnival (Carnival campero); The Blue Water Man (El fontanero azul); One Siren or Another (Unas y otras sirenas); Trial of the Virgin (Proceso a la virgen); The Minstrels (Los menestreles); The Son of Kermaria (El hijo de Kermaria); The Door (La puerta); Vision Out of the Corner of One Eye (Visión de reojo); All About Suicide (Pavada de suicidio); The Attainment of Knowledge (Para alcanzar el conocimiento); Legend of the Self-Sufficient Child (Leyenda de la criatura autosuficiente); Cat's Eye (Pantera ocular); Up Among the Eagles (Donde viven las águilas); The Place of its Quietude (El lugar de su quietud).

Side by side bilingual edition.

V2   ___. *Clara: Thirteen Short Stories and a Novel.* **Trans. Hortense Carpentier and J. Jorge Castello. New York: Harcourt Brace Jovanovich, 1976. 233 pp.**

Short Fiction:
Nihil Obstat; The Door; Trial of the Virgin; City of the Unknown; The Minstrels; The Son of Kermaria; Forsaken Woman; The Teacher; Irka of the Horses; The Legend of the Self-sufficient Creature; The Sin of the Apple; The Alphabet; A Family for Clotilde; Clara, a Novel.

V3   ___. *Open Door.* **Trans. Hortense Carpentier. San Francisco: North Point Press, 1988. 202 pp.**

Short Stories:
The Censors; The Snow White Watchman; Cat's Eye; Flea Market; Legend of the Self-Sufficient Child; Country Carnival; Generous Impediments Float Downriver; The Redtown Chronicles; Up Among the Eagles; The Attainment of Knowledge; One Siren or Another; The Blue Water Man; My Everyday Colt; Papito's Story; Strange Things Happen Here; The Best Shod; The Gift of Words; Love of Animals; The Verb *to Kill*; All About Suicide; The Celery Munchers; Vision Out of the Corner of One Eye; Ladders to Success; A Story about Greenery; The Place of Its Quietude; The Door; City of the Unknown; Nihil Obstat; A Family for Clotilde; Trial of the Virgin; The Son of Kermaria; The Minstrels.

Includes a brief preface by Luisa Valenzuela.

V4   ___. *Other Weapons.* Trans. Deborah Bonner. Hanover: Ediciones del Norte, 1985. 135 pp.

Short Stories:
Fourth Version; The Word "Killer"; Rituals of Rejection; I'm Your Horse in the Night; Other Weapons.

Includes brief bio-bibliographic notes on author by Margo Glantz and Julio Cortázar.

V5   ___. *Strange Things Happen Here. Twenty-six Short Stories and a Novel.* Trans. Helen Lane. New York and London: Harcourt Brace Jovanovich, 1986. 220 pp.

Short Fiction:
Strange Things Happen Here; The Best Shod; On the Way to the Ministry; Sursum Corda; The Gift of Words; Love of Animals; Common Transport; Vision Out of the Corner of One Eye; Porno Flick; United Rapes Unlimited; Argentina, Here Innocence is Born; The Verb *To Kill*; All About Suicide; The Zombies; Who, Me a Bum?; Neither the Most Terrifying Nor the Least Memorable; A Meaningless Story; El Es Di; Grimorium; The Celery Munchers; Ladders to Success; Void and Vacuum; A Story about Greenery; The March; Politics; The Place of Its Quietude; The Discovery; The Loss; The Journey; The Encounter.

V6   Van Steen, Edla (Brazil). *A Bag of Stories.* Trans. and intro. David George. Pittsburgh: Latin American Literary Review Press, 1991. 174

Short Stories:
Period; Good Enough to Sing in a Choir; Intimacy; The Beauty of the Lion; The Pledge; Nostalgia Row; Before the Dawn; Forever After; Apartment for Rent; CAROL head LINA heart; A Day in Three Movements; In Spite of Everything; The Return; The Misadventures of João.

V7   Van Steen, Edla, ed. *Love Stories: A Brazilian Collection.* Trans. Elizabeth Lowe. Rio de Janeiro: Grafica Editora Hamburg Ltda., 1978. 192 pp.

Short Stories:
Sonia Coutinho, Those May Afternoons. **Lygia Fagundes Telles**, Turtledove or A Love Story. **Judith Grossman**, On the Way to Eternity. **Hilda Hilst**, Agda. **Nélida Piñón**, The Shadow of the Prey. **Edla Van**

Steen, Carol Head Lina Heart

Includes an introduction by Fábio Lucas and illustrations by Italo Cencini.

V8   Vega, Ana Lydia (Puerto Rico). *True and False Romances: Stories and a Novella.* Trans. Andrés Hurley. London: Serpent's Tail, 1994. 261 pp.

Short Fictions:
Aerobics for Love; Deliverance from Evil; Solutions, Inc.; Just One Small Detail; Série Noire; Consolation Prize; Eye-Openers; Miss Florence's Trunk; *True Romances* (novella).

V9   Vélez, Diana, ed., intro., and trans. *Reclaiming Medusa: Short Stories by Contemporary Puerto Rican Women.* San Francisco: Spinsters/Aunt Lute Book Co., 1988. 161 pp.

Short Stories:
Rosario Ferré, The Youngest Doll; Sleeping Beauty; Pico Rico, Mandorico. **Carmen Lugo Filippi**, Milagros, on Mercurio Street; Pilar, Your Curls. **Mayra Montero**, Thirteen and a Turtle; Last Night at Dawn. **Carmen Valle**, Diary Entry #6; Diary Entry #1. **Ana Lydia Vega**, Three Love Aerobics; ADJ, Inc.

Includes the original Spanish versions of "Pico Rico, Mandorico" and "Thirteen and a Turtle."

X1   Xirau, Ramón, ed. "The Eye of Mexico." *Evergreen Review* 2.7 (Winter 1959): 256 pp.

Short Stories:
Guadalupe Amor (Mexico), My Mother's Bedroom.

No author information.

Y1   Yanes, Gabriela, Manuel Sorto, Horacio Castellanos Moya, and Lyn Sorto, eds. *Mirrors of War: Literature and Revolution in El Salvador.* Trans. and intro. Keith Ellis. New York: Monthly Review Press, 1985. 151 pp.

Short Fiction:
Claribel Alegría, Tamales from Cambray (and other excerpts from the novel *Izalco Ashes).*

Includes brief bio-bibliographic notes on authors.

Y2   **Yates, Donald, ed. and intro.** *Latin Blood: The Best Crime and Detective Stories of South America.* **New York: Herder & Herder, 1972. 224 pp.**

Short Stories:
María Elvira Bermúdez (Mexico), The Puzzle of the Broken Watch.

Y3   **Young, David, and Keith Hollaman, eds. and intro.** *Magical Realist Fiction: An Anthology.* **New York and London: Longman Inc., 1984. 519 pp.**

Short Stories:
María Luisa Bombal (Chile), New Islands.

Includes bio-bibliographic notes on authors.

Y4   **Young-Bruehl, Elisabeth, ed. and intro.** *Global Cultures. A Transnational Short Fiction Reader.* **Hanover: Wesleyan University Press, 1994. 509 pp.**

Short Stories:
Marta Brunet (Chile), Solitude of Blood. **Aurora Levins Morales** (Puerto Rico), El bacalao viene de más lejos y se come aquí. **Luisa Mercedes Levinson** (Argentina), The Clearing. **Carmen Lugo Filippi** (Puerto Rico), Pilar, Your Curls. **Carmen Lyra** (Costa Rica), Estefanía. **Carmen Naranjo** (Costa Rica), And We Sold the Rain. **Bertalicia Peralta** (Panama), A March Guayacán. **Cristina Peri Rossi** (Uruguay), The Influence of Edgar Allan Poe in the Poetry of Raimundo Arias.

II

Alphabetical Author Index

Number codes refer to the anthology authors and editors listed alphabetically in the Anthology Index, as well as to the authors whose works are included in those anthologies. For example, A1 is the first entry in the Anthology Index, referring to Agosín, Marjorie, the author.

Absatz, Cecilia, L3.
Agosín, Marjorie, A1, A2, A3, A4, A5, A6, C5, M16, P3.
Agüero, Omega, M18.
Aguirre, Margarita, A5, R6.
Aldunate, Elena, A5.
Alegría, Claribel, A9, A10, R6, S4, Y1.
Algandona, Lilia, J3.
Allende, Isabel, A6, A11, C2, C12, C15, C16, C17, E1, F3, G1, M6, M9, P9, R6, S10, T2.
Alonso, Dora, A4, C6, C16, E2, K3.
Alvarez, Julia, M16.
Alzola, Concepción T., S6.
Amor, Guadalupe, C18, X1.
Angel, Albalucía, F3, M10, M15, R6.
Aninat, María Flor, A5.
Antillano, Laura, M14.
Araujo, Helena, A4, C16.
Arredondo, Inés, A14, B10, M10.
Artigas, Gloria, L1.
Ayllón Soria, Virginia, B5.

Baez, Carmen, J5.
Balcells, Jacqueline, A4, A5, B1.
Bandeira Duarte, Margarida Estrela, B2.
Barrera, Luz Mercedes, J2.
Barros, Pía, A5, B3, F3, R6.
Basáñez, Carmen, A5.
Basualto, Alejandra, A5.
Bedregal, Yolanda, A4, B5, L1.
Benedetti, Giovanna, J3.
Benedetti, Lúcia, S1.
Bermúdez, María Elvira, Y2.
Bernal, Acela, J2.
Bins, Patricia, A4.
Blanco, Marta, A5, R3.
Bojunga-Nunes, Lygia, B7.1, B7.2.
Bombal, María Luisa, A4, A5, A6, A13, B8, C12, C16, F3, H7, I1, M4, M13, T3, Y3.
Bortnik, Aída, S11.
Bosco, María Angélica, L3.
Boullosa, Carmen, G2, P9.
Braschi, Giannina, B12.
Bravo, Mónica, B5.

Britton, Rosa María, J3, J4, P9.
Brunet, Marta, A4, A5, J7, Y4.
Bruzonic, Erika, B5.
Buenaño, Aminta, B5.
Buitrago, Fanny, B13.
Bulhões Carvalho da Fonseca, Emi,
    S1.
Bullrich, Silvina, F7, L3, M15.

Cabrera, Lydia, A13, B13, E1, H6,
    I1, M10, M15, P8, R6.
Calny, Eugenia, L3.
Calvimontes, Velia, L1.
Campobello, Nellie, A13, C3.
Campos, Julieta, C4, P8, P9, R6.
Cárdenas, Magolo, L7.
Cartagena Portalatín, Aída, E1, E2,
    F4, L7.
Casanova, Cecilia, R3.
Castedo, Elena, A5, F2, P9.
Castellanos, Rosario, A7, A12, C8,
    C16, F7, G1, I1, M10, M15.
Castillejos Peral, Silvia, J2.
Cerda, Marta, B10, P9.
Cevasco, Gaby, B5.
Chávez-Vásque, Gloria, C10.
Chehade Durán, Nayla, L1.
Chiriboga, Luz Argentina, B11.
Clavel, Ana, J2.
Cohen, Regina, J2.
Colasanti, Marina, S1.
Collado, Delfina, J3.
Conde Zambada, Hilda Rosina, J2.
Contreras, Hilma, E2, F4, M18.
Correia Dutra, Lia, S1.
Coutinho, Sonia, S1, V7.
Cruz, Soledad, F4.

da Fonseca, Cristina, A5.
Dávila, Amparo, C16, M10, M12,
    M15.
Daviú, Matilde, F3, L7.
de Crespo, Elda L.C., M17.
De Fokes, María Asunción, A5.

de Jesús, Carolina María, A13, B14,
    G4.
de la Parra, Teresa, A13, M14, R7.
de Queiroz, Rachel, A13, C12, G6,
    M7, M10, S1.
de Quiroga, Giancarla, B5.
de Vallbona, Rima, C16, D4, E1, J3,
    P4, R2, U1.
del Castillo, Laura, P11.
del Río, Ana María, A5, R6.
Denser, Márcia, S1.
Di Giorgio, Marosa, A6.
Diaconú, Alina, A6.
Díaz-Diocaretz, Miriam, G4.
Diez Fierro, Silvia, L1.
Dolores, Carmen, G3, S1.
Dorado de Revilla Valenzuela, Elsa,
    B5
dos Santos, Estela, D5.
Dueñas, Guadalupe, B10, C18, T3.
Dughi, Pilar, B5.
Dujovne Ortiz, Alicia, P3.
Dupré, Leandro Sra., S1.

Eltit, Diamela, C9, P9.
Engle, Margarita, M16.
Escudos, Jacinta, S4.
Estenssoro, María Virginia, C16.
Estrada, Josefina, J2.

Fagundes Telles, Lygia, A4, C9,
    C12, C13, C15, E1, F1, M10,
    R6, S1, V7.
Fanaro, Silvia, R4.
Farias, Alejandra, A5.
Fernándes de Oliveira, Cicera, G4.
Fernández Moreno, Inés, L1.
Ferré, Rosario, A13, B6, C12, C15,
    C16, E1, E2, F4, F5, F6, G1, I1,
    J1, M14, M15, M18, P5, P9,
    V9.
Fort, María Rosa, C5.
Fox, Lucía, E1.
França, Aline, B14.

Martín, Rita, B4.
Martínez, Nela, B5.
Mastretta, Angeles, B10, G2, P9.
Matto de Turner, Clorinda, A13, J6.
Maturana, Andrea, L1.
Mellet, Viviana, L1.
Mendoza, María Luisa, F3.
Mistral, Gabriela, A3, C12, D1, D2,
    F7, H7, R7.
Molina, Silvia, B10, G2, R6.
Molloy, Sylvia, R6.
Montecinos, Sonia, A5.
Montero, Mayra, F4, V9.
Mujica, Barbara, A5, C5.
Muñiz (Muñiz-Huberman),
    Angelina, M15, M20, S11.

Naranjo, Carmen, A4, C16, J3, J4,
    N1, P4, P7, P8, P9, R2, R6, S4,
    U1, Y4.
Nery, Adalgisa, S1.
Niemeyer, Margarita, A5.
Nolla, Olga, E2, F4, R6.

Ocampo, Silvina, A4, A6, B9, C9,
    C12, D5, F3, K4, L3, M5, M10,
    M15, O1, R6.
Ocampo, Victoria, C9, M15.
Odio, Eunice, J3, U1.
O'hara, Maricarmen, O2.
Oreamuno, Yolanda, J3, R2, U1.
Orfanoz, Luz, A5.
Orozco, Olga, A6, C16.
Orphée, Elvira, A4, A6, C9, P8.
Ortiz Cofer, Judith, M16, S3.
Ortiz Salas, Mónica, B5.

Palacios, Antonia, C16.
Pallotini, Renata, F3.
Partnoy, Alicia, D7, P2.
Paz, Blanca Elena, B5.
Peralta, Bertalicia, J3, J4, P4, P5,
    S4, Y4.
Pereira, Teresinka, P6.

Peri Rossi, Cristina, A4, A6, A13
    C2, C9, C16, F3, I1, M1, M15,
    P3, P7, R6, Y4.
Pinto, Julieta, J3, J4, R2.
Piñón, Nélida, A4, A13, C9, C12,
    C16, I1, M15, P8, R5, R6, S1,
    S7, V7.
Pizarnik, Alejandra, A6, F3, G5,
    M10, M11.
Pizarro, Ana, A5.
Pla, Josefina, C16.
Poletti, Syria, L3, P10.
Poniatowska, Elena, A4, A13, B10,
    C16, E1, F3, J5, M9, M10, P9.
Porzecanski, Teresa, C16, K1, K2.
Puga, María Luisa, B10, C2, G2,
    R6.

Quevedo, Violeta, A5.

Rendic, Amalia, A4, A5.
Reyna, Bessy, F2, J3, P4.
Riesco, Laura, A4, B5.
Robles, Mireya, M16.
Rodríguez, Aleida, G4.
Roffé, Reina, L3.
Roffiel, Rosamaría, F3.
Rojas Sucre, Graciela, J3, M17.
Romo-Carmona, Mariana, G4.
Rosel, Sara, G4.
Rossel Huicí, Gladys, B5.

Sala, Mariella, R6.
São Paulo Penna e Costa, Marília,
    G6.
Saris, Lake, G4.
Seligson, Esther, K1, S11.
Shua, Ana María, A6, L1.
Silva Ossa, María, R1.
Silveira de Queiroz, Dinah, G6, H7,
    M10, S1.
Simo, Ana María, C6, C14.
Solá, Marcel, A6.
Solari, María Teresa, C16.

III

Author by Country Index

Number codes refer to the anthology authors and editors listed alphabetically in the Anthology Index, as well as to the authors whose works are included in those anthologies. For example, A1 is the first entry in the Anthology Index, referring to Agosín, Marjorie, the author.

Argentina
Absatz, Cecilia, L3.
Bortnik, Aída, S11.
Bosco, María Angélica, L3.
Bullrich, Silvina, F7, L3, M15.
Calny, Eugenia, L3.
del Castillo, Laura, P11.
Diaconú, Alina, A6.
dos Santos, Estela, D5.
Dujovne Ortiz, Alicia, P3.
Fernández Moreno, Inés, L1.
Futoransky, Luisa, K2.
Gallardo, Sara, A6.
Glickman, Nora, C16, F2.
Gorodischer, Angélica, A6, E1, M10, R6.
Guido, Beatriz, F3, L2, M10.
Hecker (Heker), Liliana, A6, C16, H4, M8, M9, M10, M12.
Heer, Liliana, D5.
Heker (Hecker), Liliana, A6, C16, H4, M8, M9, M10, M12.
Herrera, Matilde, R6.
Ingenieros, Delia, B9, K4.

Jamilis, Amalia, L3.
Kociancich, Vlady, C16, M10, P9, S7, T4.
Lange, Norah, C9.
Laurini, Myriam, P1.
Levinson, Luisa Mercedes, A6, C16, L2, L3, M15, Y4.
Lynch, Marta, L3, M10, M15.
Malinow, Inés, M15.
Molina, Silvia, B10, G2, R6.
Molloy, Sylvia, R6.
Ocampo, Silvina, A4, A6, B9, C9, C12, D5, F3, K4, L3, M5, M10, M15, O1, R6.
Ocampo, Victoria, C9, M15.
Orozco, Olga, A6, C16.
Orphée, Elvira, A4, A6, C9, P8.
Partnoy, Alicia, D7, P2.
Pizarnik, Alejandra, A6, F3, G5, M10, M11.
Poletti, Syria, L3, P10.
Roffé, Reina, L3.
Shua, Ana María, A6, L1.
Solá, Marcela, A6.

IV

Title Index

Number codes refer to the anthology authors and editors listed alphabetically in the Anthology Index, as well as to the authors whose works are included in those anthologies. For example, A1 is the first entry in the Anthology Index, referring to Agosín, Marjorie, the author.

When the title of a story also appears in Spanish, this indicates that it is published bilingually. Stories appearing in more than one anthology may show slight variations in their titles. All stories are printed here as they appear in the anthologies.

Rene, Claribel Alegría, A10.
Report on Heaven and Hell, Silvina
 Ocampo, O1.
Requiem for a Wreathless Corpse,
 Olga Nolla, F4.
Requiem for Solitude, Giannina
 Braschi, B12.
Residuum, Luisa Mercedes
 Levinson, L2.
The Resurrection of the Flesh,
 Angélica Gorodischer, A6.
Retrospection, Angelina Muñiz-
 Huberman, M20.
The Return, Edla Van Steen, V6.
Revelation, Silvina Ocampo, O1.
The Revelation, Cristina Peri Rossi,
 P7.
Revenge, Marjorie Agosín, A2.
Revenge, Isabel Allende, A8.
Rice and Milk, Rosario Ferré, F3.
The Ring, Eugenia Viteri, B5.
Río de la Plata, Marjorie Agosín,
 A1.
Rising, Mournful from the Earth,
 Angelina Muñiz, M15, M20.
Rituals of Rejection, Luisa
 Valenzuela, V4.
Rivers, Marjorie Agosín, A1, A2.
The Road North, Isabel Allende,
 A11.
Roads of the Mirror, Alejandra
 Pizarnik, G5.
Roque's Via Crucis, Claribel Alegría,
 A10.
Rosa the Beautiful (excerpt from *The
 House of the Spirits*), Isabel
 Allende, P8.
Routine Inspection, Pía Barros, B3.
The Rubber Tree, Marjorie Agosín,
 A1.
The Rupture, Elena Poniatowska,
 P9.
Ruth v. the Torturer, Alicia Partnoy,
 D7.

Ruth's Father, Alicia Partnoy, P2.
Sabotage, Alicia Yánez Cossío, I1,
 M15.
Sailing Down the Rhine, Sonia
 Guralnik, A5.
The Sailor's Wife, Silvia Diez Fierro,
 L1.
Salarrue, Claribel Alegría, A10.
Salicio and Amarylis, Angelina
 Muñiz-Huberman, M20.
The Sarcasm of God, Angelina
 Muñiz-Huberman, M20.
Sargasso, Marjorie Agosín, A1.
The Sauna, Lygia Fagundes Telles,
 C9, F1.
The Scent of Violets, Giovanna
 Benedetti, J3.
Scents of Wood and Silence, Pía
 Barros, A5, R6.
The Schoolteacher's Guest, Isabel
 Allende, A11.
The 'Screaming Bag,' Maricarmen
 O'hara, O2.
The Sea, Gabriela Mistral, A3.
The Seamstress from Saint
 Petersburg, Marjorie Agosín,
 A1.
The Secret, María Luisa Bombal,
 A5.
The Secret Life of Grandma
 Anacleta, Rima de Vallbona,
 D4.
The Secret World of Grandmamma
 Anacleta, Rima de Vallbona,
 E1.
The Seed Necklace, Rosario Ferré,
 F6.
Segismundo's Better World, Alicia
 Steimberg, A6.
Self Denial, Silvina Bullrich, L3.
Seña Paula, Elda L. C. de Crespo,
 M17.
The Señorita Didn't Teach Me,
 Bethzabé Guevara, B5.

Symbiotic Encounter, Carmen
Naranjo, C16.

Takeover, Beatriz Guido, L3.
Taking the Vows, Claribel Alegría,
A10.
The Tale of the Velvet Pillows,
Marta Traba, C16.
The Tales of My Aunt Panchita,
Carmen Lyra, D3.
The Tales of My Aunt Panchita
(prologue), Carmen Lyra, A13.
Tales of the Struggle in Northern
Mexico (excerpt from
Cartridge), Nellie Campobello,
A13.
The Talisman (novella), Claribel
Alegría, A9.
Tamales from Cambray (excerpt
from the novel *Izalco Ashes*),
Claribel Alegría, Y1.
Tangerine Girl, Rachel de Queiroz,
C12.
Tangible Absence (excerpt from
*Texts of Shadow and Last
Poems*), Alejandra Pizarnik,
G5.
Tango, Luisa Valenzuela, R6.
Tapihue, (from *Silendra*), Elizabeth
Subercaseaux, A6.
Tarciso, Dinah Silveira de Queiroz,
H7.
Tarma, María Rosa Fort, C5.
The Taste of Good Fortune, Acela
Bernal, J2.
Tatabisako, Lydia Cabrera, P7.
The Teacher, Armonía Somers, S2.
The Teacher, Luisa Valenzuela, S2,
V2.
Telepathy, Alicia Partnoy, P2.
Tell Me a Story, Olo, Carmen
Naranjo, N1.
Temptation, Clarice Lispector, L5.
Temptress of the Torch-Pines, Gloria

Velázquez, G2.
Ten Times Around the Block,
Beatriz Guido, L3.
Tenebrae Service (excerpt from
Oficio de tinieblas), Rosario
Castellanos, A12.
Teresa Irene, Angela Hernández,
P9.
The Termites (Las termitas), Gloria
Chávez-Vásquez, C10.
Terra incognita (excerpt from same),
Victoria Ocampo, C9.
That's Where I'm Going, Clarice
Lispector, L6.
There Never Was a Once Upon a
Time, Carmen Naranjo, N1.
They Called Her Aurora (A Passion
for Donna Summer), Aída
Cartagena, E2.
Things, Silvina Ocampo, A6.
The Things that Happen to Men in
New York!, Giannina Braschi,
B12.
The Thirsty Little Fish, Jacqueline
Balcells, B1.
Thirteen and a Turtle, Mayra
Montero, V9.
This Love, Marjorie Agosín, A2.
This Noise Was Different, Rosario
Ferré, F4.
Those May Afternoons, Sonia
Coutinho, V7.
Three Days, Luisa Valenzuela, C1.
Three Knots in the Net, Rosario
Castellanos, A7, A12.
Three Love Aerobics, Ana Lydia
Vega, V9.
The Three Marías (excerpt), Rachel
de Queiroz, A13.
The Threshold, Cristina Peri Rossi,
P7.
Thus Were Their Faces, Silvina
Ocampo, A6, O1.
Tickle of Love, Marjorie Agosín,

V

Authors and Their Works Index

Number codes refer to the anthology authors and editors listed alphabetically in the Anthology Index, as well as to the authors whose works are included in those anthologies. For example, A1 is the first entry in the Anthology Index, referring to Agosín, Marjorie, the author.

When the title of a story also appears in Spanish, this indicates that it is published bilingually. Stories appearing in more than one anthology may show slight variations in their titles. All stories are printed here as they appear in the anthologies.

Absatz, Cecilia
A Ballet for Girls, L3.

Agosín, Marjorie
A Huge Black Umbrella, C5.
A Recent Nakedness, A2.
A Scented Love Letter, A2.
Adelina, A1.
Alfama, A2.
Allison, A2.
The Alphabet, A2.
An Immense Black Umbrella, A1.
Beds, A1.
Birthday, A2.
Blood, A1.
The Blue Teacups, P3.
Bonfires, A2.
The Bottle, A2.
Bougainvillaea Insomnia, A2.

Braids, A1.
Cartographies, A1.
Chepita, A2.
Chocolates, A2.
The Color Black, A2.
Convents, A2.
Cousins, A2.
The Dead Death Sounds, A2.
Distant Root of Autumn Loves, A1.
Dreamer of Fishes, A2.
The Dreams of Van Gogh, A1.
Dunedin, A2.
Emma, A1.
Fat, A1.
The Fiesta, A1.
First Communion, A2.
First Time to the Sea, A1.
Forests, A1.
The Gold Bracelet, A1.

Works Cited: Bibliographies of Latin American Literature in Translation

Alarcón, Norma, and Sylvia Kossnar. *Bibliography of Hispanic Women Writers.* Bloomington: Chicano-Riqueño Studies, 1980.

Balderston, Daniel. *The Latin American Short Story: An Annotated Guide to Anthologies and Criticism.* New York: Greenwood Press, 1992.

Brazilian Authors Translated Abroad. Rio de Janeiro: Fundaçao Biblioteca Nacional, Ministerio da Cultura, Departamento Nacional do Livro, 1994.

Bryant, Shasta M. *A Selective Bibliography of Bibliographies of Hispanic American Literature.* Austin: Institute of Latin American Studies. The University of Texas Press at Austin, 1976.

Corvalán, Graciela. *Latin American Women in English Translation: A Bibliography.* Los Angeles: Latin American Studies Center, 1980.

Freudenthal, Juan R., and Patricia M. Freudenthal, eds. *Index to Anthologies of Latin American Literature in English Translation.* Boston: G.K. Hall and Co., 1977.

Hulet, Claude L., ed. *Latin American Prose in English Translation. A Bibliography.* Washington, D.C.: Pan American Union, 1964.

Jamieson, Sally Brewster. *English Translation of Latin American Literature: A Bibliography.* Washington, D.C.: Pan American Union, Division of Intellectual Cooperation, 1947.

Kanellos Nicolas, ed. *Biographical Dictionary of Hispanic Literature in the United States: The Literature of Puerto Ricans, Cuban Americans, and Other Hispanic Writers.* New York: Greenwood Press, 1989.

Latin American Writers in English Translation: A Tentative Bibliography. Washington, D.C.: Pan American Union, 1944.

Levine, Suzanne Jill. *Latin American Fiction and Poetry in Translation.* New York: Center for Inter-American Relations, 1970.

Marting, Diane, ed. *Spanish American Women Writers: A Bio-bibliographical Source Book.* New York: Greenwood Press, 1990.

___. *Women Writers of Spanish America: An Annotated Bio-bibliographic Guide.* New York: Greenwood Press, 1987.

Phelan, Marion. *A Bibliography of Latin American Fiction in English.* Phoenix: Latin America Area Research, 1956.

Porter, Dorothy B. *Afro-Braziliana: A Working Bibliography.* Boston: G.K. Hall & Co., 1978.

Resnick, Margery, and Isabelle de Courtivron, eds. *Women Writers in Translation. An Annotated Bibliography, 1945-1982.* New York and London: Garland Publishing, Inc., 1984.

Shaw, Bradley A., ed. *Latin American Literature in English Translation. An Annotated Bibliography.* New York: New York University Press, 1976.

Stern, Irwing, ed. *Dictionary of Brazilian Literature.* New York: Greenwood Press, 1988.

Vásquez, Carmen. "Bibliographical Resume of English Translations." *Cultural Identity in Latin America.* Ed. Birgitta Leander. Paris: UNESCO, 1986: 201-4.

Wilgus, Kana S., ed. *Latin American Books. An Annotated Bibliography.* New York: Center for Inter-American Relations, 1974.

Wilson, Jason, ed. *An A to Z of Modern Latin American Literature in English Translation.* London: The Institute of Latin American Studies, 1989.

___. "Spanish American Literature in Translation." *SLAS Bulletin* 22, Jan. 1975: 14-18.

Zimmerman, Marc. *U.S. Latino Literature: An Essay and Annotated Bibliography.* Chicago: March/Abrazo Press, 1992.

About the Compiler

KATHY S. LEONARD is Associate Professor of Spanish and Hispanic Linguistics at Iowa State University. She has published two anthologies of edited and translated short stories by Latin American women, and her work has appeared in such journals as *Feminist Studies*, *Michigan Quarterly*, and *Critical Matrix: The Princeton Journal of Women, Gender, and Culture*.

ISBN 0-313-30046-1

90000

EAN

9 780313 300462